FORMS OF AID

BENEDICT CLOUETTE
MARLISA WISE

FORMS OF AID

Architectures of Humanitarian Space

Birkhäuser Basel

TABLE OF CONTENTS

1. The Spaces of “Humanitarian Space”

In theorizing the operational arena of international relief organizations in the early 1990s, Rony Brauman, the former director of Médicins Sans Frontières, offered a new definition, the concept of *humanitarian space*. Humanitarian space, as articulated by Brauman, is a non-partisan sphere of operations, decision-making, access, and movement for relief organizations, where they are "free to evaluate needs, free to monitor the delivery and use of assistance, free to have dialogue with the people."[1] Key to Brauman's definition is the political independence and neutrality, at least in theory, of the institutions, technologies, and actors that participate in humanitarian operations. The concept of humanitarian space implies the separation of a moral imperative oriented toward the preservation of life and the lessening of human suffering, as distinct from the civil, political concerns of the state or the parties to a conflict.

1 Brauman did not coin the term, but provided a theoretical basis that continues to condition its use. *Humanitarian space* was already used by the UNHCR in the context of Cold War–era conflicts in Central America during the 1980s. See the report by Sarah Collinson and Samir Elhawary, *Humanitarian Space: A Review of Trends and Issues* (London: Overseas Development Institute, 2012).

Humanitarian space is animated around the category of the human, particularly the human who can no longer rely on the intercession of the state to protect them and preserve their life. Humanitarian space is thus the territory corresponding to a kind of antisovereignty, a space that may be geographically located within and yet is legally and conceptually outside, or even opposed to, the territory of the state. Humanitarian space is the antimatter of sovereignty. It is a space in which decisions over life and its value are guided by the apolitical, moral reason of humanitarianism, theoretically independent of and indifferent to the reason of the state. Unlike the presumed fixity of the state within its borders, humanitarian space is a mobile and shifting field that shrinks and grows with the activities of aid workers.

Brauman's *humanitarian space* has influenced similar articulations of the space of humanitarianism, such as the term *humanitarian operating environment* preferred by the UN Office for the Coordination of Humanitarian Affairs (OCHA). In its definition of the term, OCHA stresses that "the perception of adherence to the key operating principles of neutrality and impartiality in humanitarian operations represents the critical means by which the prime objective of ensuring that suffering must be met wherever it is found, can be achieved."[2] The definition acknowledges something that every humanitarian worker knows, that it is not neutrality per se that is at stake, but rather the performance and perception of neutrality, the maintenance of which secures access to affected populations, independent of the political allegiances of the relief organizations or those they seek to help.

2 OCHA, *Glossary of Humanitarian Terms in Relation to the Protection of Civilians in Armed Conflict* (New York: OCHA, 2003).

This definition exposes a tension between humanitarian reason and action: the invocation of humanity as a universal and apolitical category orienting humanitarian action is less a matter of logical consistency than it is a pragmatic claim. Whether or not it is theoretically valid, the definition of humanitarian space in practice is aimed at producing an effect within a field of powerful actors by asserting the impartiality of humanitarian organizations, and thereby guaranteeing their safe and continued access to populations determined to be in need of their assistance. The concept of humanitarian space removes humanitarian organizations from the violence of political struggles onto the plane of morality, shifting their work to a different register in which it is accountable not to the interests of the powerful but only to the human as a universal, disinterested, and apolitical form of life.

The assertion of humanitarian space is therefore an act of savoir faire: it mobilizes an expedient concept to give cover to the activities of organizations in situations where the conditions of urgency, confusion, and danger seem to require a term that creates a space in which certain actions are recognized as being above the fray of politics. Humanitarian action is subject to a different regime of justification and accountability, insofar as it cares for humans in the moment of their abandonment by the state, by their neighbors and kin, in short, by anything that takes an interest in them as particular or individual lives, or as citizens. Humanitarian space, as a claim, is justified through the effects it produces, by its outcomes and efficacy, as humanitarian activity often is. Regardless of whether the concept of humanitarian space is considered valid in theory, its productivity is undeniable, in that it conditions the possibilities of action and the evaluation of consequences within particular concrete situations. It does not so much describe an existing condition as it creates and sustains a space by dictating how that space should be understood as well as the norms of conduct and the obligations of actors within that space.

In that sense, humanitarian space is an intangible concept that has concrete results. It is a rhetorical construct that does something spatially; specifically, it makes and holds space for the operations of humanitarians and their organizations. But the instrumentality of the term within specific situations on the ground has a consequence: that in producing the concept of humanitarian space as a universal sphere of activity, it must nonetheless embed itself within particular spatial relationships, which is to say, political relationships. Humanitarian space is an antiterritory, a universal space that exceeds national boundaries but produces highly specific spatial consequences in the cities and regions that it temporarily incorporates. In responding to disasters and conflicts in the name of humanity, contemporary humanitarianism has engendered new urban forms, often through the convergence of nongovernmental actors with economic, military-security, and national interests.

A watchtower unit sits atop a Palestinian building near Shuhada Street in Hebron, where the ground-floor commercial spaces have been shuttered by the IDF as a security precaution, which has devastated the local economy.

As architects, it is these forms, the spaces of humanitarian space, that are our concern, in that they suggest the contours of international humanitarianism as it is practiced and as it reorders cities around the world. Or rather, as it reorders, at times, parts of cities, and at other times, a larger geographical terrain; indeed, the presumed universality of humanitarian space allows it a slippery relationship to scale. Working on and through several scales simultaneously, the effects of humanitarian space, like the effects of the economic and national interests that it temporarily displaces, are unevenly distributed and highly contingent on local political factors that determine the particular subsection of humanity and the specific spaces on which humanitarianism acts. We therefore will consider humanitarian space through the urban and architectural effects that it produces as it reshapes cities in the areas that it temporarily integrates into its logics.

Sovereignty

The end of the Cold War made possible a broadening of the conditions under which humanitarian missions could be undertaken in many parts of the world. Countries whose sovereignty was previously guaranteed by their strategic significance to a superpower were left with diminished geopolitical leverage after the breakup of the Soviet Union. Furthermore, the breakup itself produced ethnic and political violence in countries that had been part of or aligned with the Soviet Union. The result was a dramatic expansion of the role of the UN as the body charged with enforcing international and humanitarian law, increasingly through military action. Between 1988 and 1998, the UN authorized and deployed thirty-five peacekeeping missions, compared with zero in the previous ten-year period, and only thirteen in the earlier history of the UN since its founding in 1948.[3]

3 Tamara Duffey, "Cultural Issues in Contemporary Peacekeeping," *International Peacekeeping* 7, no. 1 (2000): 142–68.

Throughout these years, the mandates for humanitarian operations broadened, and began to increasingly converge with international security agendas. The UN Operation in Somalia (UNOSOM), a peacekeeping mission from 1993 to 1995, was an early example of a new role for the UN, in which ground troops were sent to ensure that humanitarian aid would be delivered to the intended recipients. The UN withdrew in 1995 following heavy casualties with no central government in place, but the mission was a turning point in the role of the UN as both a key humanitarian actor in the post-1992 era and as a military force authorized to act in the interests of global security, as defined by the member nations of the UN Peacebuilding Commission.

This tendency of converging humanitarian and military interests was established and reinforced by a series of interventions in the 1990s. In addition to the UN's operations in Somalia, which were carried out with additional forces from the US military, the UN undertook prominent peacekeeping missions in Rwanda, the former Yugoslavia, Liberia, Sudan, Côte d'Ivoire, Sierra Leone, the Congo, and elsewhere. In the same period, powerful nations, sometimes in coalitions, expanded the precedent of humanitarian-military interventions operating outside a UN mandate. The US bombed Serbian positions around Sarajevo with the justification of preventing further casualties during the siege of the city, and the British sent troops to Sierra Leone, in both instances without authorization from the UN. The US-led bombing of Kosovo by NATO and France's intervention in Côte d'Ivoire continued this trend of nation-states offering humanitarian justifications for military interventions.

In the same period, humanitarian organizations increasingly operated in active war zones and, to some extent, set political agendas in the locales in which they were working, deepening the dominance of northern international NGOs. Somalia was also the first instance in which the International Committee of the Red Cross (ICRC) employed private security forces, which points to the different nature of the conflict in which the ICRC was operating, in which the violence of the Somali civil war was no longer limited to parties that were signatories to international law.[4]

4 Alex de Waal, "Humanitarianism Reconfigured: Philanthropic Globalization and the New Solidarity," in *Nongovernmental Politics*, ed. Michel Feher (New York: Zone Books, 2007).

The international legal framework used to justify interventions was a novel political invention of the last decade of the twentieth century, often referred to as "the right to intervene." Indeed, the UN Charter, adopted after World War II, had specifically asserted the "sovereign equality" of member states, and proscribed intervention in domestic matters of foreign countries, essentially upholding principles of state sovereignty in the European legal tradition dating, at least mythically if not in practice, to the Peace of Westphalia of 1648 and the theories of the Swiss jurist Emer de Vattel's *The Law of Nations* (*Le Droit des Gens*, 1758). On the contrary, the right to intervene, developed in response to Rwanda and other atrocities of the early 1990s, suggested that states could justify military action in other nations in the name of humanity, effectively abrogating considerations of sovereignty when states commit grave human rights abuses, genocide, and crimes against humanity, or fail to protect their citizens from such violence. The right to intervene is the contemporary basis of international humanitarianism as a form of anti-sovereignty, or, more positively, a nonstate sovereignty.

The difficulty posed by the right to intervene was that it made intervention an option at the disposal of powerful states while providing no guidelines that would oblige a consistent response to comparable circumstances, thereby creating a tension between sovereignty and humanitarian concerns. The failure of the international community to respond more quickly to the genocide in Kosovo is often cited as a result of framing intervention as a "right" that can be exercised or not at the discretion of states, making it highly dependent on political exigencies rather than the moral calculus of humanitarianism.

In response to the increasingly complex contexts in which the UN and NGOs were operating and the uneven results of those missions, a set of guidelines was developed by the International Commission on Intervention and State Sovereignty (ICISS), a high-level international committee set up by the Canadian government at the prompting of UN Secretary-General Kofi Annan. The Commission issued its recommendations in December 2001 in a report titled "The Responsibility to Protect." The report shifted the criteria for humanitarian intervention from a right to intervene, the previous framework, to asserting that it was not only a right, but the duty of the international community to send peacekeepers to countries in instances when the state cannot provide for the safety of its citizens. The committee's report suggested that the criteria compelling intervention included not only civil wars and human rights abuses but also natural disasters. The doctrine was adopted by the UN in 2005, albeit in a modified form that dropped natural disasters and instead focused on the state's responsibility to protect its population from crimes against humanity, genocide, and rights abuses.

R2P (Responsibility to Protect) was initially hailed by international affairs experts as a positive step in guaranteeing global security. But in practice, R2P has been only partially upheld, in part because its reliance on the military power of the US has become a liability after the failed nation-building efforts following the Iraq and Afghanistan wars. Most recently, the hesitancy of the US and other Western powers to intervene in Syria has demonstrated the limits of R2P. Meanwhile, the increasing power of China and Russia in world affairs, two countries that have been historically reluctant to endorse humanitarian interventions and who occupy permanent seats on the UN Security Council, has reintroduced the possibility that the long-heralded waning of state sovereignty may be reversed in the current decade.[5]

5 Jayshree Bajoria and Robert McMahon, "The Dilemma of Humanitarian Intervention," The Council on Foreign Relations, last updated June 12, 2013, goo.gl/iuakzM.

NGOs and Humanitarian Government

At the same time that the UN and its member states were redefining the relationship of humanitarian imperatives to state sovereignty, nongovernmental organizations were becoming increasingly powerful in both domestic and international politics. The anthropologist Didier Fassin dates the dawn of this "second humanitarian era" to the founding of Médicins Sans Frontières (MSF) in 1971. The group of doctors who founded MSF broke from the International Committee of the Red Cross (ICRC) over their objections to the ICRC's official neutrality in the face of atrocities committed during the Biafran War. Where the ICRC's impartiality and recognition by international bodies had allowed them a near-monopoly on providing medical aid to conflict areas in the earlier part of the century, MSF lay claim to organizational independence on the basis of its willingness to testify against state power in the name of humanitarian principles.[6]

6 Didier Fassin, "Humanitarianism: A Nongovernmental Government," in Feher, *Nongovernmental Politics*, 150 (see note 4).

The history of MSF, and the larger movement of "sans frontières" international NGOs to which it gave rise, points to the uneasy relationship between state and nonstate actors in their claims to represent the human. MSF's emphasis on witnessing and testimony orients their actions as independent of, and potentially against, the state, by caring for the human in the face of state violence. This orientation became increasingly necessary in the context of peacekeeping operations, the humanitarian-military interventions that conceptually conjoined the preservation of life with the exercise of violence, and the alignment of humanitarianism with global security in the 1990s. International NGOs offer a moral counterbalance to state reason even as they remain dependent on states and their militaries for protection and logistical support to carry out their operations.

The interdependence of state and nongovernmental organizations in the administration of aid characterizes what Fassin terms *humanitarian government*, which works not only across national borders, but on the very boundaries between state and nonstate formations by invoking humanity as the basis of a moral order.[7] NGOs are internationalized at the same time that states are "humanitarianized," drawing symbolic capital from the virtuous actions of NGOs to underwrite their commitments to their population, not, or not only, as citizens, but as humans. The result is a form of international humanitarian order that is sustained through the coordinated activities of governments and NGOs, as well as a rhetorical and legal interplay between them that confers virtue on sovereign power to the extent that it upholds human rights and protects human life, and conversely denounces the state and conceptually suspends sovereignty in claiming a humanitarian space when it fails to do so.

7 Ibid, 151.

The close proximity of governmental and nongovernmental organizations in the administration of humanitarian missions leads to the ambiguity of whether the US Marines landing in Mogadishu, Somalia, in 1992 were, in Alex de Waal's terms, the "vanguard of the humanitarian international, or the shock troops of philanthropic imperialism." De Waal calls the post-Cold War period the era of "humanitarianism unbound," in which the mobility and borderlessness of humanitarian organizations, both governmental and nongovernmental, became a new norm. The explosion of international NGOs in the countries of the northern hemisphere led to an increasing influence of solidarity politics, through which civil society groups could exert pressure on the democratic governments of their home nations to adopt diplomatic agendas that embraced a humanitarian role for powerful northern states. The politics of these NGOs varies widely, from the liberal, universalist human-rights mission of Amnesty International to geographically focused student organizations promoting international responses to regional crises such as Save Darfur, to issue-based organizations like Feed the Children, and specialists in a particular technical service, such as MSF or Ingénieurs Sans Frontières (ISF). In the United States, the rise of evangelical organizations such as World Vision International led to the unusual alliance between the administration of George W. Bush and African governments, resulting in more money being given to fight AIDS in Africa during his presidency than in any previous administration.

The gate at the entrance to a health clinic in Kibera, Nairobi, operated by Médecins Sans Frontières.

From the work of the ICRC in World War I, operating under a highly delimited mission of providing life-saving aid to injured soldiers on the battlefield to the vast constellation of NGOs working internationally in the twenty-first century, an expansion can be observed. It is not only an expansion of the geographical space of NGOs operating increasingly across borders, both within and against the state, it is also an expansion of the mandate of humanitarian organizations to act not only to save lives in war, but to ameliorate poverty, to provide food and access to health care, shelter, water, and sanitation, a whole realm of activity that was previously considered the purview of international human development, or the responsibility of the state. For example, MSF operates a clinic in Kibera, a slum in Nairobi, that provides free inpatient and outpatient services, maternity care, and pediatric medicine to local residents. The increasing overlap between humanitarianism and developmentalism could be understood in a positive light, as a shift from the treatment of the symptoms of conflict and violence to their causes in poverty, inequality, and insecurity. But it also brings humanitarian groups into relationships of complicity with organizations that promote international economic development. As we will see, aid to human development can take the form of funding for factories that manufacture goods for multinational corporations in deregulated "free zones," allowing companies tax-free access to countries with low-cost labor and loose regulations. The expansion of the mission of humanitarian organizations to include activities and alliances more commonly understood as developmentalist while at the same time operating in coordination with military-security organizations suggests a potential antinomy in the universality of humanitarianism as it aligns with economic liberalism and international security, in that it ties altruistic motivations to particular interests even as it claims a moral authority in the name of humanity.

In the field of architecture, the mantle of the "sans frontières" was, until recently, most prominently assumed by Architecture for Humanity (AFH), the US-based charity founded in 1999 by Cameron Sinclair and Kate Stohr. During its fifteen years in operation, AFH sought to leverage the energy and knowledge of (mostly young) architects from across many (mostly northern hemisphere) countries to develop architectural solutions to humanitarian crises, ranging from civil wars to natural disasters. The organization was founded in response to the need for housing to shelter refugees returning to Kosovo at the end of the Balkans conflict, and went on to support the design and construction of buildings as part of the reconstruction of areas of India and Sri Lanka after the 2004 tsunami, the US Gulf Coast after Hurricane Katrina in 2005, Haiti after the 2010 earthquake, housing for internally displaced persons (IDPs) in Afghanistan and Sudan, and schools in several West African nations. At the height of AFH's influence, Sinclair invoked the "between four and five billion people on the planet who are looking for my help," comparing these "clients" to the small handful of people in the world who could commission an architect like Zaha Hadid.[8] Of course, Sinclair's clients were not humanity as a whole but the particular NGOs, companies, and national governments that fund AFH's projects, a point that became evident with the demise of the organization in 2015 as a result of insufficient funding.[9]

8 Sinclair quoted in Lucy Siegle, "Give Me a Shelter," *The Guardian*, May 14, 2006, goo.gl/lieKZ5.

9 This point was made by Laura Kurgan in a discussion in *Volume* magazine. See "Design Like You Give a Damn: A Conversation with Kenneth Frampton, Michael Bell, and Laura Kurgan," *Volume* 10 (2006): 112–15.

In architecture, as in other fields, the invocation of a universal humanity often obscures the political and economic relationships without which effective humanitarian action would be impossible. The alibi provided by "humanitarian space" may be useful in shifting the motives and justifications for decisions to the plane of a moral imperative, and doing so can indeed provide access to resources, funding, and political power that would be inaccessible to more explicitly interested enterprises. Nevertheless, humanitarian space—in the sense that we use the term—is defined not by the conceptual isolation of a pure, universal humanity, but by a series of topological relationships between state and nonstate actors, citizens and humans, interest and altruism, particular and universal, local and global, politics and morality.

The spatial corollary of humanitarianism is perhaps not humanitarian space as defined by Brauman as an impartial sphere of relief activity, but rather a topological inversion, or, in Giorgio Agamben's terms, an inclusive exclusion, a space that is simultaneously embedded within and conceptually and legally outside the space of politics, the territory of the state.[10] Humanitarian space is extraterritorial.

10 Giorgio Agamben, *Homo Sacer: Sovereign Power and Bare Life* (Stanford: Stanford University Press, 1998).

Extraterritoriality

Recent considerations of the *zone* in architectural and spatial theory have drawn attention to this spatiojuridical loophole as a recurrent feature of international urban development. Keller Easterling's work presents a particularly insightful and sustained analysis of the free zone—in its various acronymic guises of the FEZ, SEZ, EPZ, IPZ, and QIZ—as a repeatable "spatial product" that smooths the circulation of capital as it is rerouted through international switch-points, or what we previously called cities. Easterling has introduced the zone as part of a cast of spatial actors that together perform what she terms *extrastatecraft*, the exercise of an agile power over space that bypasses or exceeds the state and its territorial limits.[11]

11 Keller Easterling, *Extrastatecraft: The Power of Infrastructure Space* (New York: Verso Books, 2014).

In considering the architectural and spatial consequences of humanitarian operations, the affinities between humanitarian space and other forms of extraterritoriality, like the zone, become recognizable. The concept of humanitarian space makes a claim to a kind of extraterritoriality, insofar as it postulates a space corresponding to a responsibility that exceeds the legal relation of the state to its citizens.

Humanitarian space frequently aligns with and overlies extraterritorial spaces. The most well-known example is the land on which the UN's four headquarters are built, which are geographically located in New York, Geneva, Vienna, and Nairobi, but legally hold extraterritorial status, governed by international law rather than the local jurisdiction. And yet the extraterritoriality of humanitarianism is not limited to the land parcels occupied by international diplomatic organizations. As our research in Haiti, the West Bank, and Kenya suggests, the relationship between sites of humanitarian operations and extraterritorial spaces is extensive and multifaceted.

Indeed, free zones are implicated in the extraterritoriality of humanitarian space. The zone exists outside the customs territory of its host country, which allows it a greater degree of integration, or at least points of alignment, with organizations that extend across borders, whether multinational corporations, NGOs, or UN agencies. Haiti's Cité Soleil, the most prominent slum in Port-au-Prince and the site of sustained battles with the UN peacekeeping force MINUSTAH, started as a social housing project that was initially planned as accommodations for workers in the nearby export processing zone (EPZ). Decades later, the same EPZ received official development aid through acts of the US Congress, both before and after the earthquake, nominally in support of the country's rebuilding, but also to maintain access to tax-free manufacturing labor and facilities for American garment companies. Similarly, the growth of the Mukuru slum in Nairobi, now one of the city's largest, was driven in part by the Kenyan government's development of an industrial zone, and later the tax-free Sameer Industrial Park EPZ, on the edge of the city, near the airport. Mukuru's earliest residents were workers who voluntarily resettled in areas adjacent to the zone to be closer to the factories and the possibilities of employment they offer. The Sameer Industrial Park currently houses the Kenyan warehouses of Médicins Sans Frontières, and its EPZ leases space to several companies that are international distributors of relief supplies, the same as are used by the UN and NGOs in their work in Kenya's slums. In the West Bank, the settlement of Ma'ale Adumim, which is currently the focus of efforts by the right wing in the Israeli Parliament to annex territory east of Jerusalem, was first developed as residences for workers in an adjacent industrial park, Mishor Adumim, in the 1970s.[12] The companies in Mishor Adumim, almost all of which are owned by Israelis, receive special tax breaks under Israeli law even though the area is not legally recognized as Israeli territory, and today most of the labor in the industrial zone is drawn from nearby Palestinian towns.[13] The expropriation of Palestinian land to create a free zone is one of the many spatial techniques that Israeli settlers have used over the years to exploit the multiple jurisdictions and territorial ambiguities of the West Bank.

12 "Israel's Hard-liners want to 'Go Big': Annex a Settlement," *New York Times*, January 17, 2017, goo.gl/I7Vtd6.

13 "Down the Road from SodaStream, A Complicated Coexistence," *Ha'aretz*, January 30, 2014, goo.gl/Vhcof1.

Nature reserves are another figure of extraterritorial space that sometimes coincide with the spaces of humanitarian operations. In Nairobi, the Kibera slum is built on land that was originally an "ethnic reserve" for Nubian soldiers during the British colonial era and that became a national forest after independence. The status of the land, initially under semiautonomous administration by the Nubians and then later appropriated as public property, remains a source of conflict and continues to impede attempts to normalize land tenure for residents of the slum. In the West Bank, the Israel Nature and Parks Authority has recently declared two new national parks in East Jerusalem, imposing limitations on Palestinian development and access to these lands for farming and other uses, and incorporating those areas into the municipality of Jerusalem.[14] Here, the nature reserve is not so much an extraterritorial space but rather a reterritorialization of previously disputed land that works through an appeal to the universal values of environmental protection and heritage conservation.

14 "Israel Moves to Build East Jerusalem Park, Despite Pending Final Approval," *Ha'aretz*, January 11, 2012, goo.gl/tOwjZc. See also the report mentioned in the article by Bimkom, "From Public to National: National Parks in East Jerusalem," goo.gl/enWe3E.

It is certainly not the case that humanitarian operations are ineluctably linked to free zones, policies of economic liberalization, or the land grabs of colonial powers through appeals to universal human values. Nor do zones in themselves inevitably lead to slums, dislocation, political instability, or other markers of a humanitarian crisis. Rather, both the zone and humanitarian space are related effects of a transition in state sovereignty in the last decades that is marked by a shifting balance of international political power, an increasingly globalized economy, and an expanded mandate for international organizations to intervene in civil conflicts in the interest of global security and the protection of human rights. Much of the literature on the supposed crisis of sovereignty has focused on the effects of economic globalization and liberalization—and the free zone as their spatial analogy—but international humanitarianism has also prompted reconsiderations of sovereignty through its own form of extraterritoriality in the conceptual figure of humanitarian space, as well as through the practices of humanitarian organizations and their effects on the planning and administration of cities. The shifting status of state sovereignty since the end of the Cold War has enabled humanitarian operations to influence the planning and construction of cities around the world, in ways that architects and urbanists have not yet fully appreciated.

Spatial Techniques of Separation and Incorporation

The techniques through which humanitarian space is configured reinforce the topological inversion, the extraterritoriality of an inclusive exclusion.

A gated area near the National Palace complex in Port-au-Prince, Haiti, encloses a tent camp built in the wake of the 2010 earthquake.

Walls and borders separate humanitarian space from civic life, while their gates and checkpoints regulate the movement of people and supplies across their boundaries. Towers, an archetypal form of optical surveillance, project power across a terrain, incorporating and organizing it along lines of vision and weaponry, even as they divide friend from enemy. Parks, both industrial zones and nature preserves, introduce an alien space in the city, while simultaneously marking that space as foreign and unassimilable. The shelters provided by humanitarian organizations offer relief from homelessness and space for daily routines, even as they resist resettlement of their populations in the host city. These techniques comprise a spatial repertoire and a series of architectural forms that negotiate the inclusive exclusion.

While we draw the figure of the inclusive exclusion from Agamben, we emphasize a different valence in that topology than he seems to appreciate. The inseparability of humanitarian space from the space of the city, its irreducible attachments to political and economic interests, and its inclusion in spite of its exclusion are the preconditions for a return to the polis from the camp. Humanitarianism, far from apolitical, is premised on the recognition of the biopolitical basis of civil relationships. Refugees cannot be reduced to pure humanity—bare life, in Agamben's terms, or Hannah Arendt's stateless people. Humanitarian space is already the exercise of an antisovereignty on the lives of noncitizens whose existence in a territory that is not theirs nonetheless represents the potential for the emergence of new forms of political life.

TYPOLOGIES
Wall

1.

2.

1. A swing mounted on the Israeli side of a concrete barrier that was built to block off a part of Hebron's Old City to Palestinians 2. The perimeter wall of a Médecins Sans Frontières clinic in Port-au-Prince

3.

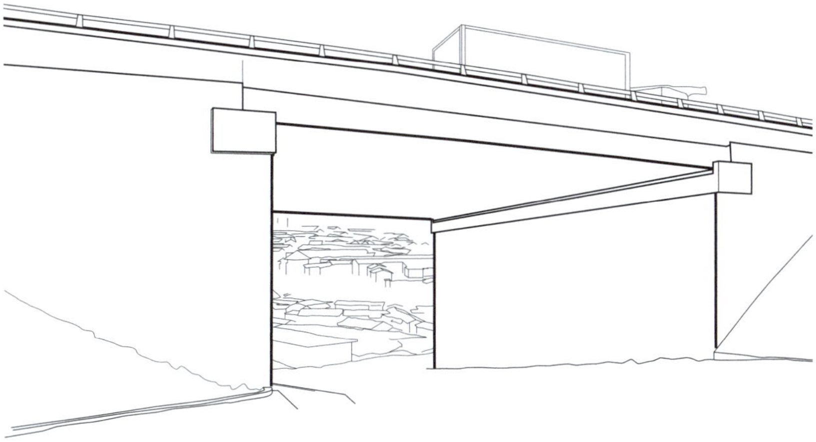

4.

3. A segment of the Israeli West Bank Separation Barrier (sometimes known as the Apartheid Wall) near Checkpoint 300 at Rachel's Tomb, as approached from Bethlehem 4. An overpass on Nairobi's Southern Bypass Road, separating Kibera from the Decanting Site

Highway 60

The Israeli Highway 60 is the main north–south route through the West Bank, serving both Palestinian and Israeli communities while contributing to the fragmentation of the landscape and prevention of a future Palestinian state. At the location shown here, the entrance to the Israeli settlement El'azar, Highway 60 is open to both Israeli and Palestinian drivers, but it is closed to green (Palestinian) plates north and south of Jerusalem, and is closed to yellow (Israeli) plates through Jenin.

SONAPI perimeter wall

The wall that surrounds SONAPI's boundaries follows the edges of major roads and is a dominant visual feature of the landscape near the airport and industrial zone of downtown Port-au-Prince. Punctuated at several points by guard posts and towers, the wall is regulated both by private security officers verifying credentials and monitoring the flow of workers, and by MINUSTAH soldiers, who were engaged to prevent labor uprisings at SONAPI following protests in 2009. The wall is only passable to workers in the manufacturing facilities, dividing the zone from the rest of the city.

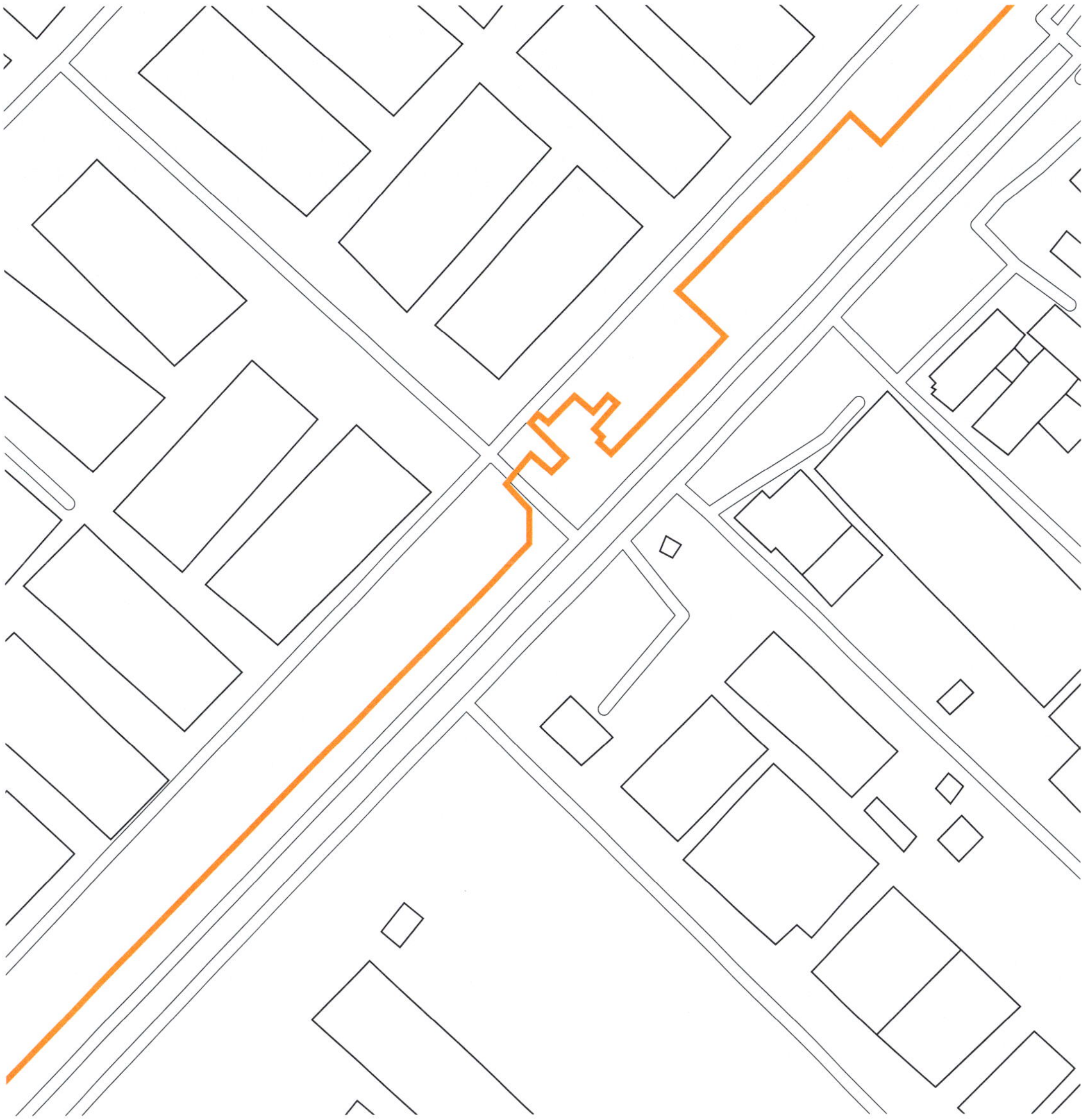

Kibera Railroad

Owned by the Kenya Railways Corporation (KRC), the tracks cut a dangerous barrier through the center of Kibera, which has grown up around the tracks over decades of self-built construction efforts. There have been periodic clearance efforts by KRC to widen the space around the tracks, resulting in lost homes and investments for residents, and also tragic accidents as when a cargo train derailed in December 2013 and crashed into homes built close to the rail tracks.

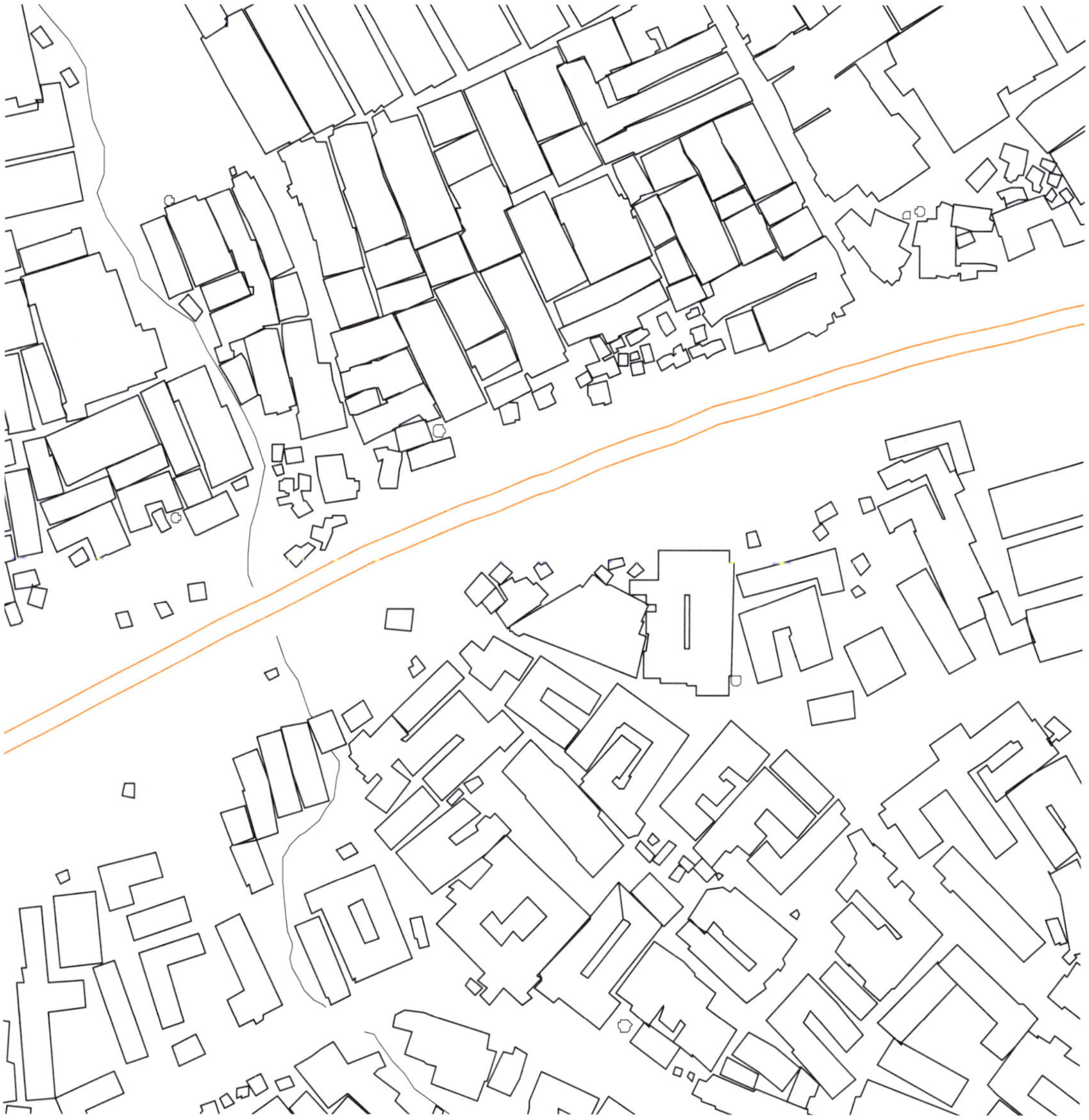

Southern Bypass Road between KENSUP and Kibera

The newly relocated residents of the housing built by the Kenya Slum Upgrading Programme (KENSUP) are separated from their families and communities remaining in Kibera by housing policies and design that discourage economic and social interactions. To limit the pirating of utility networks, residents of Kibera are not allowed within the boundaries of the KENSUP site, which prevents vendors in the housing from selling to the much larger pool of residents in Kibera, creating a social and economic barrier between the housing and the settlement. The Southern Bypass Road, a highway that connects Nairobi's western suburbs to its central business district, adds a further physical obstruction between the new housing and Kibera.

Israeli Separation Wall

The wall which runs through the West Bank separating Israeli and Palestinian communities is variously referred to as the "separation barrier" and the "apartheid wall," among other names. It does not correspond with any agreed-upon border, and its material qualities and dimensions shift along its length in response to political pressures. According to B'Tselem, the full route of the wall (including built portions, portions under construction, and those in the planning stages) is 709 kilometers long, twice as long as the Green Line. The wall is shown here at the northern outskirts of Bethlehem, where Checkpoint 300 and Rachel's Tomb distort and open gates into the barrier. Rachel's Tomb, a site of religious tourism, is accessible only to those arriving from the Israeli side of the wall. Checkpoint 300, inaugurated in 2005, was the first checkpoint constructed in the separation wall and has the atmosphere and procedures of a crossing at an international border, often crowded in the early-morning hours with long lines of Palestinian workers passing through for work on the Israeli side of the wall.

TYPOLOGIES
Tower

1.

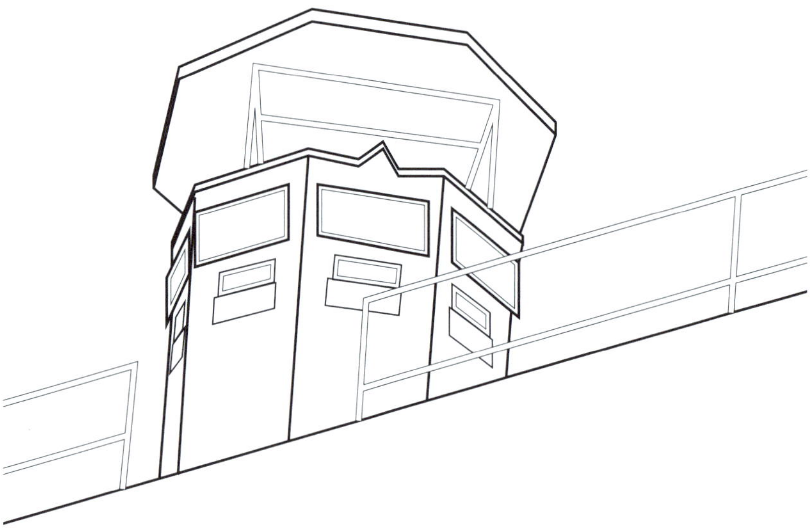

2.

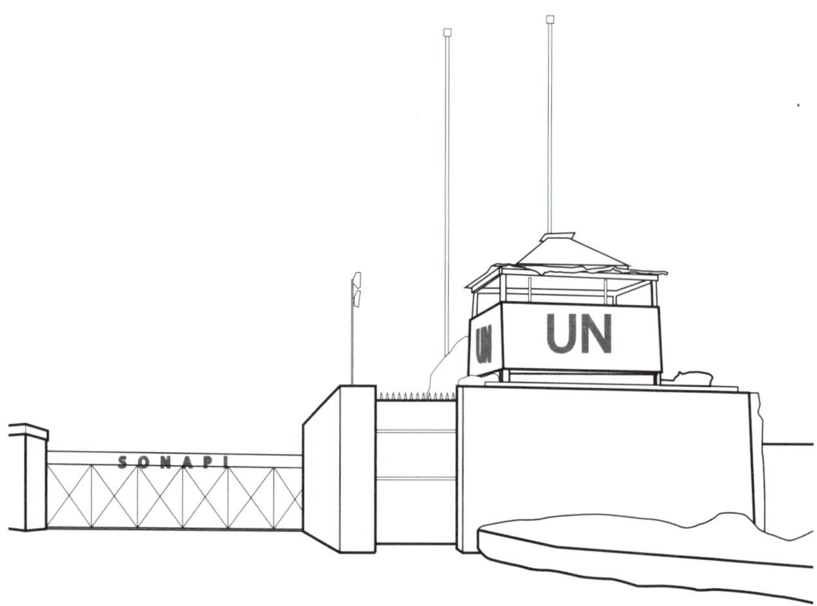

1. An Israeli Defense Forces guard tower on the roof of an Israeli settlement inside the Old City of Hebron 2. A UN guard tower at the gate of the SONAPI EPZ in Port-au-Prince

3.

4.

3. The UN-Habitat field office in Kibera, near the entrance of the settlement 4. A water and sanitation station in Kibera, built by the NGO Umandi Trust, which has a toilet on the first floor and an observation deck on the top level

Blue House

Since 2004 MINUSTAH has occupied Cité Soleil by force (in numbers greater than the entire Haitian National Police) with the mandate "to restore a secure and stable environment" after the exile of Jean-Bertrand Aristide. At major entry points, MINUSTAH occupies buildings as guard posts and checkpoints, maintaining visual surveillance from the upper levels of the buildings. Shown here is the Blue House, a former gang stronghold seized by MINUSTAH and converted to a surveillance tower and base of operations. The structure collapsed during the earthquake in 2010, taking the lives of ten Brazilian MINUSTAH soldiers.

MINUSTAH guard post at SONAPI

SONAPI is guarded at all entry points, and since the labor strikes of August 2009, badges have been implemented to identify individual workers and their affiliations with trade unions banned by the owners of SONAPI factories, a policy seemingly in conflict with the labor organizing protections included in the Haitian Hemispheric Opportunity through Partnership Encouragement Act of 2006 (HOPE) legislation, which provides substantial funding to the owners of the textile companies operating within SONAPI. The highlighted guard tower is staffed by armed MINUSTAH troops, and painted with a large UN logo that is visible from a long distance.

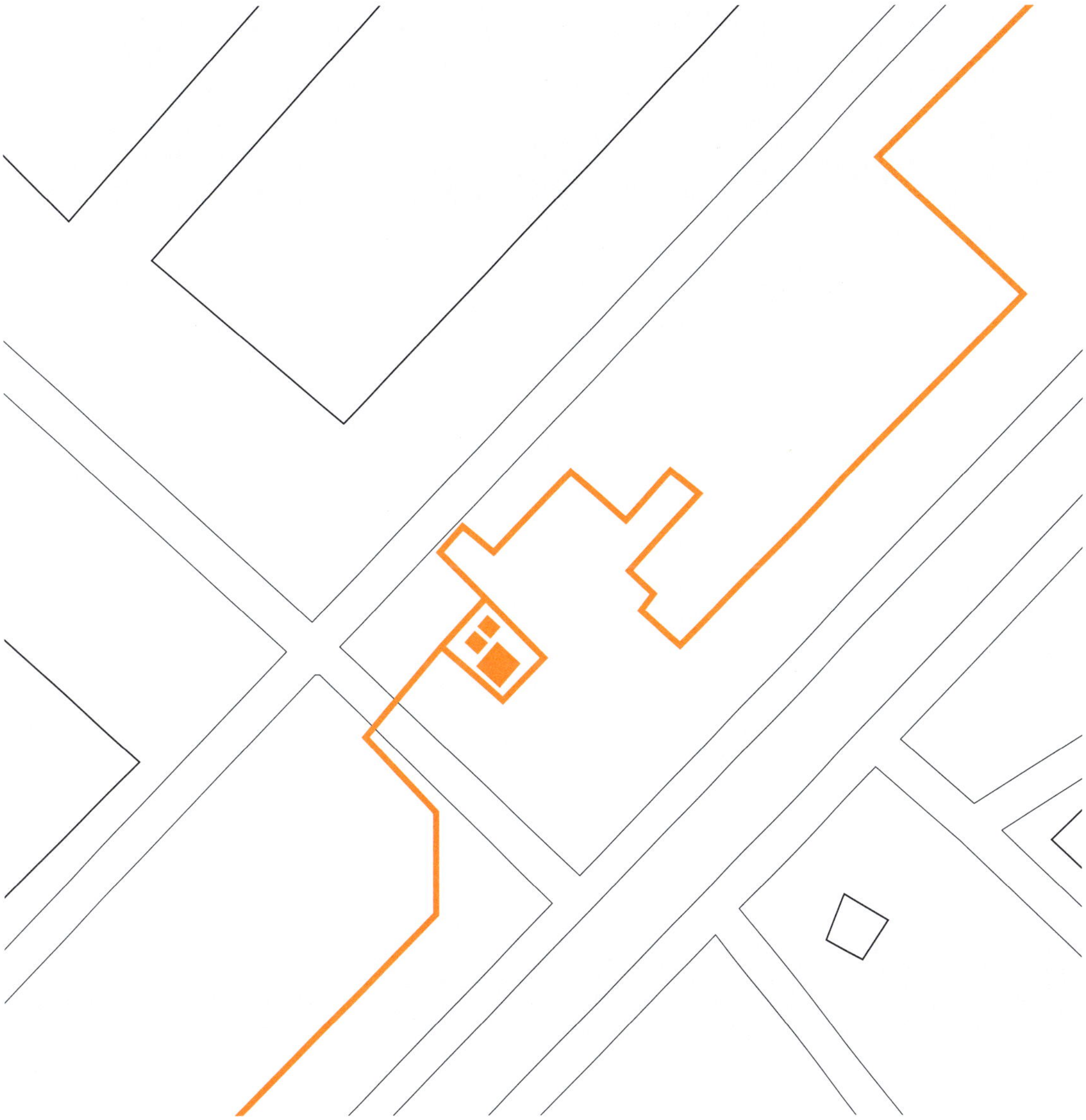

Tosha 1 biogas tower

Built in 2007, Tosha 1 was the first biogas center in Kenya, and uses digital identification cards to increase security along with a cashless payment system to reduce burglary attacks. The two-level facility houses bathrooms and toilets on the first floor, and the upper level has open windows providing a panoramic view over Kibera. Partner agencies on the project include Umande Trust, the Halcrow Foundation, Athi Water Services Board, Nairobi City Water and Sewerage Company, and the Swedish International Development Cooperation Agency. According to the Umande Trust, the tower is sited on community land, and thus subject to the same land tenure conflicts as all buildings in Kibera.

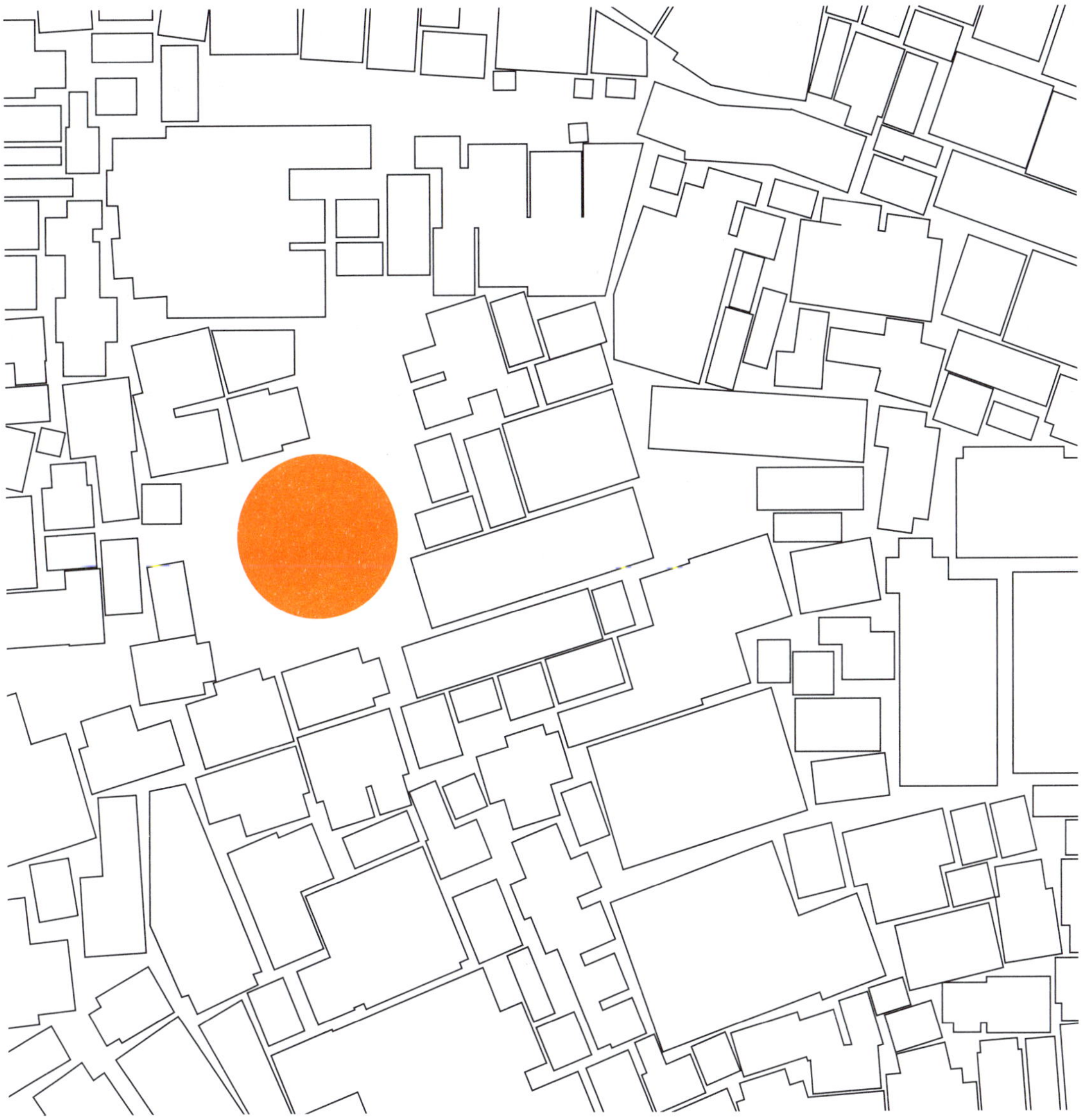

UN field office, Kibera

Located on the road leading into Kibera from Mbagathi Way, adjacent to the Nyayo Highrise Estate and Riara University, this small UN-Habitat office consists of two stacked shipping containers sited in an enclosed yard. The compound also includes the offices of the Settlement Executive Committee (SEC). When we visited for the first time, we met with members of the SEC, who tried to insist that we pay them to provide an armed security escort to guarantee safe travel through the settlement. We declined, as we had already made arrangements to be met by other contacts who were residents of Kibera.

Gush Etzion highway tower

Gush Etzion Junction marks the entrance to the Etzion Bloc settlements in the West Bank and is located at the intersection of Route 367 and Highway 60. It has been the site of numerous acts of violence and assault, including ten attacks during two months in the fall of 2015. A large, heavily fortified tower sits on the southwest corner of the junction, with panoramic, operable strip windows and an array of security cameras mounted on the roof. Additional smaller guard posts at ground level are hemmed in by protective concrete barriers that leave only a small area of glazing exposed for surveillance.

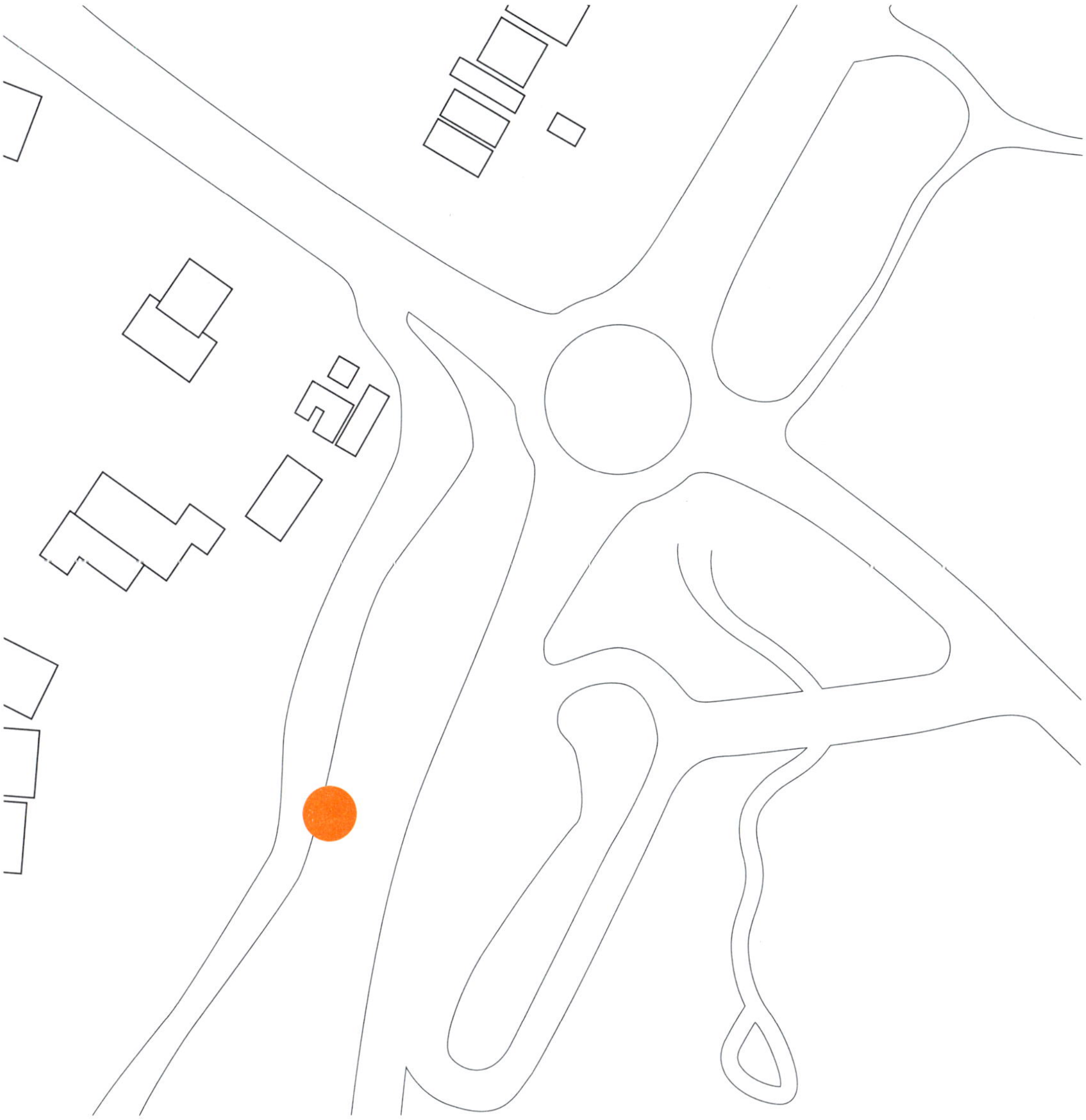

Beit Romano settlement rooftop guard towers

The Beit Romano settlement within Hebron is largely constituted by the Yeshiva Shavei Hevron and the IDF military post which protects it. In 2002 the Israeli High Court of Justice blocked the construction of additional student dorms in the settlement, a decision that was reversed in 2008. The walled settlement is surrounded by numerous watchtowers on the roofs of buildings within the settlement as well as abutting Palestinian buildings, and is adjacent to the heavily militarized Shuhada Street.

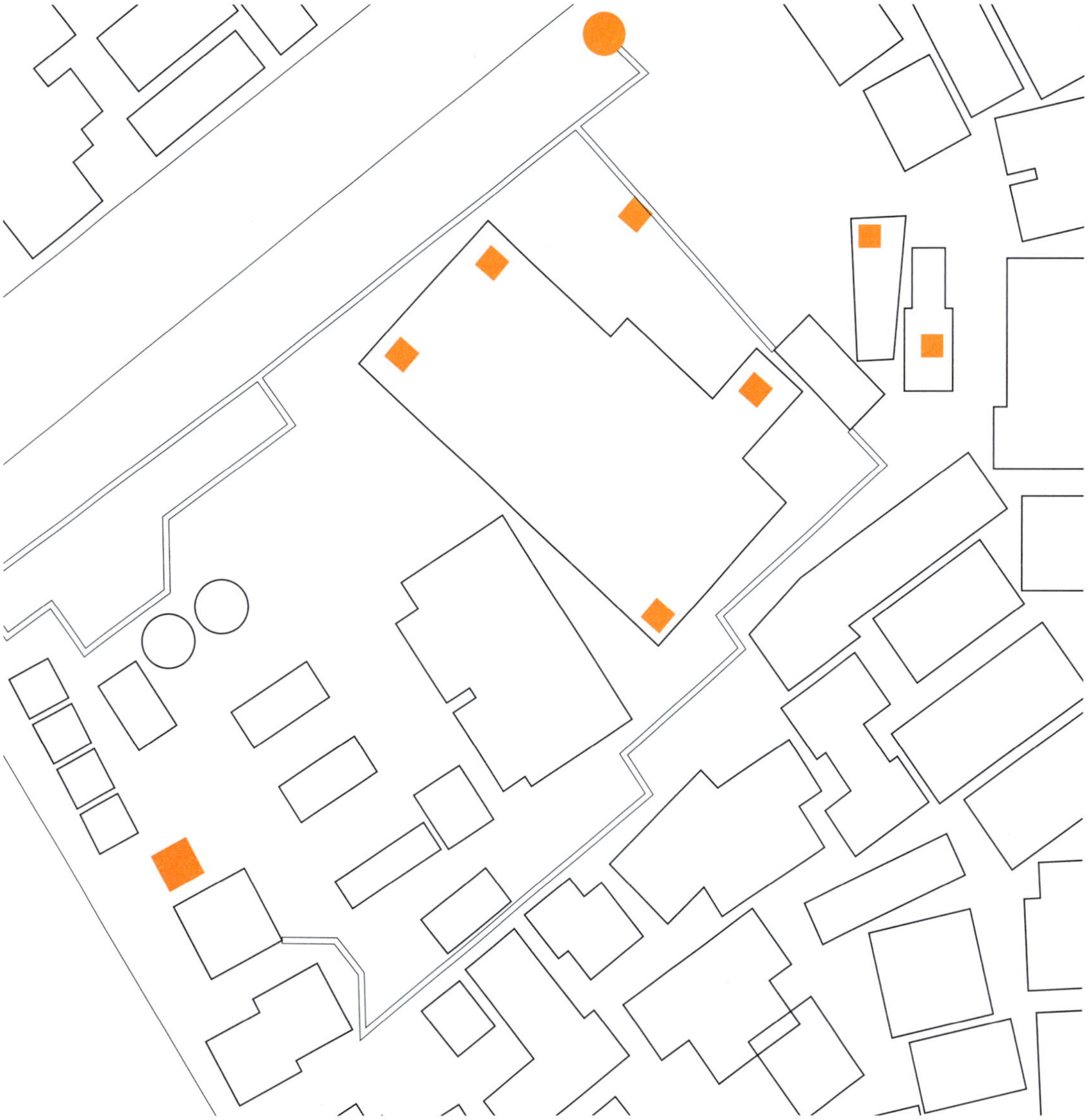

41

TYPOLOGIES
Shelter

1.

2.

1. Self-built structures in a tent camp in Port-au-Prince incorporate tree branches, earthquake debris, and tarps bearing the logos of aid organizations 2. Masonry residential towers at the Decanting Site adjacent to Kibera, Nairobi

3.

4.

3. A wattle-and-daub residential structure in Kibera, Nairobi 4. A multi-family masonry building in the El-Azar settlement, West Bank

Cité Soleil self-built housing

Founded in 1958 by President François Duvalier, Cité Soleil was originally designed to house manual laborers for the local Export Processing Zone and was a beacon for rural migrants seeking employment in the urban factories being constructed in the 1960s. The UN-led embargo of the early 1990s sent the export industry into a spiral, worsening conditions in Cité Soleil. After the 2010 earthquake, reports stated that it took two weeks for relief aid to reach the community despite its centralized position between the airport and marine port. The lightweight materials of many self-built houses resulted in less damage than in neighborhoods dominated by concrete block houses.

45

Place Fierté IDP camp

The housing in Cité Soleil fared relatively well in the earthquake of 2010, being largely constructed of lightweight and flexible materials like corrugated metal and wood, with only some buildings made of heavier materials like concrete masonry units. Those who lost their homes became refugees, internally displaced in an area known as the worst slum in the hemisphere, and were moved to a tent camp in Place Fierté. The camp swelled to the borders of the park and was supported by numerous aid groups, including Yele, founded by rapper Wyclef Jean, before it was cleared in 2012.

El'azar settlement housing

The quasi-suburban housing in El'azar may not look like shelters provided by aid organizations, but construction and maintenance are heavily funded by international nonprofit groups assisting the settlements in the Etzion Bloc. Residents receive substantial subsidies including immigration and resettlement assistance, tax breaks, mortgage benefits, and incentives from the Israeli government, while additional funds are raised in the US and directed to the settlement by the Gush Etzion Foundation and other charities via tax-deductible donations. El'azar was originally founded by American Jews and remains engaged in diaspora politics, embedded in an international network of fundraising and charity organizations.

49

KENSUP housing

A joint project of the Kenyan Ministry of Housing and UN-Habitat, the Kenya Slum Upgrading Programme (KENSUP) was initiated as a means to fast-track the achievement of the Millennium Development Goals in a highly visible location. KENSUP has targeted Kibera as the proving ground for participatory slum upgrading projects (PSUPs), but as of 2015 had built only 600 units at a reported cost of $11,000 USD each. At such a slow rate, it would take thousands of years to house Kibera's population, based on midrange estimates.

Kibera self-built housing

A number of housing forms were made illegal when Kibera was declared "unauthorized" in 1963. Building codes outlaw the use of permanent building materials like brick and concrete, effectively prohibiting residents from improving their living conditions. The codes also forbid the installation of infrastructure such as electricity or water by the residents, exacerbating dangerous living conditions in the area. A 2002 report made in the preparatory phase of the UN's slum upgrading program demonstrated that 57 percent of landlords in the slum are either government officers or politicians who exploit Kibera's "unauthorized" status for economic gain.

Dheisheh housing

Following the 1948 Arab-Israeli War, residents of forty-five Palestinian villages were offered temporary refuge in Dheisheh by UNRWA on land that the agency had leased from Jordan. Thirty-four hundred people moved into tents covering 0.31 km^2, intending to return home as soon as possible. In the late 1950s UNRWA built 10 m^2 single-room concrete units as more permanent housing, a move which was initially resisted by the refugees. Yet sixty years later, the camp has expanded on the original shelter units and grown to a population of 13,000 living on the original 0.31 km^2. Many of the refugees continue to insist on their right of return to the original forty-five villages, and the ever-expanding and solidifying camp is simultaneously denied and created by its residents.

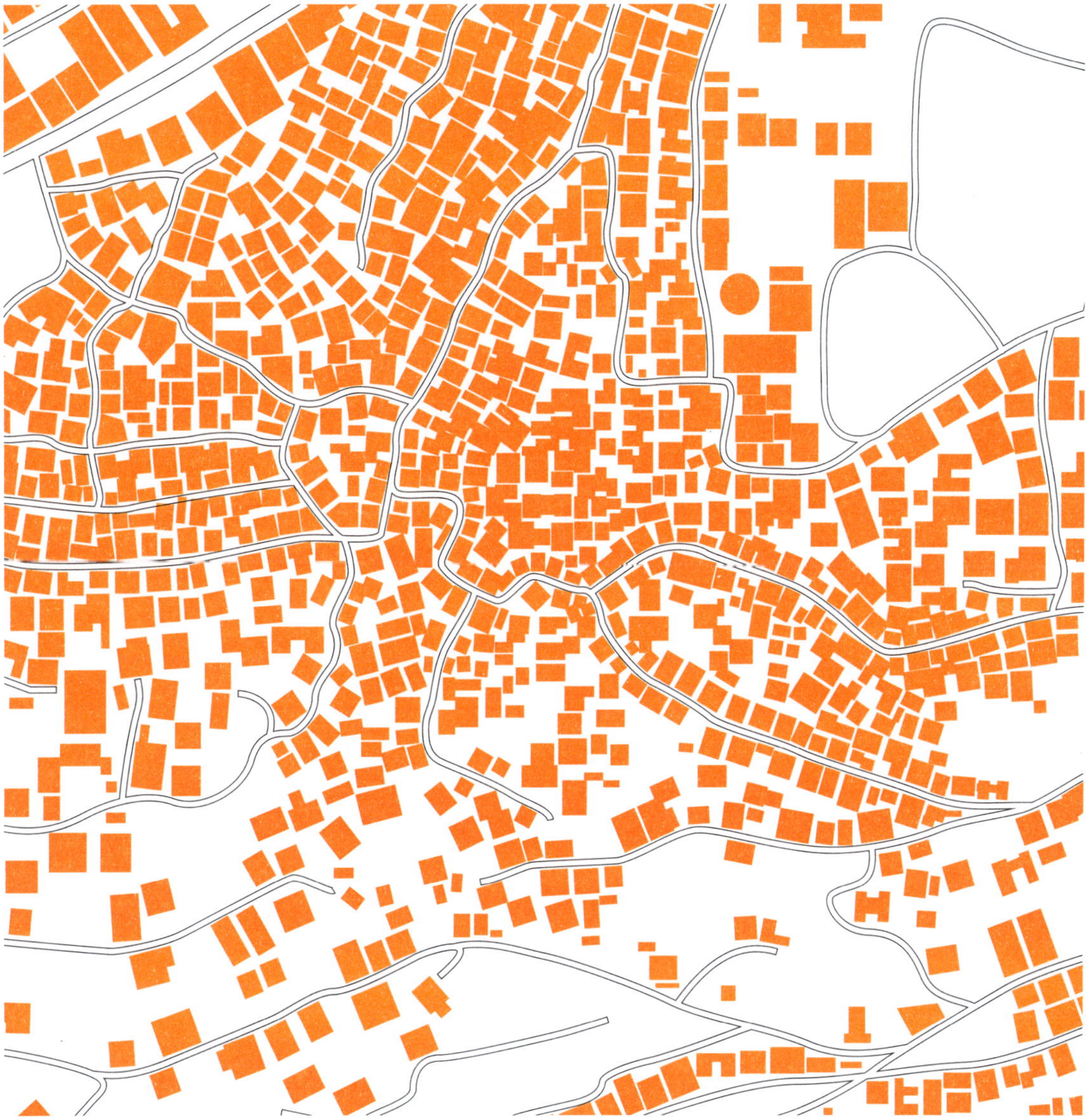

TYPOLOGIES

Park

1.

1. A public plaza built by the Hebron Rehabilitation Committee with funding from international donors, in the Old City of Hebron

2.

3.

2. Kibera, a settlement in Nairobi built on land that is now designated as a national forest
3. The Sameer Industrial Park EPZ and the ICRC Logistics Center in Nairobi

Place Fierté

Once a rare resource of public space in an incredibly dense community, the Cité Soleil park became home to more than 1,000 IDPs between 2010 and 2012. Previously a place of recreation for the underserved community, the IDP camp filled the park across the street from the Brazilian MINUSTAH compound. The border of the park signaled the spatial demarcation between slum dwellers and refugees, the politicized poor under military occupation and the humanitarian subjects administered by aid organizations. After the clearance of the camp in 2012, MINUSTAH, along with the Community Violence Reduction and Civil Affairs Sections, announced the start of a $190,000 project to rehabilitate the existing basketball courts, construct a multipurpose community center, improve general landscaping, and plant indigenous trees.

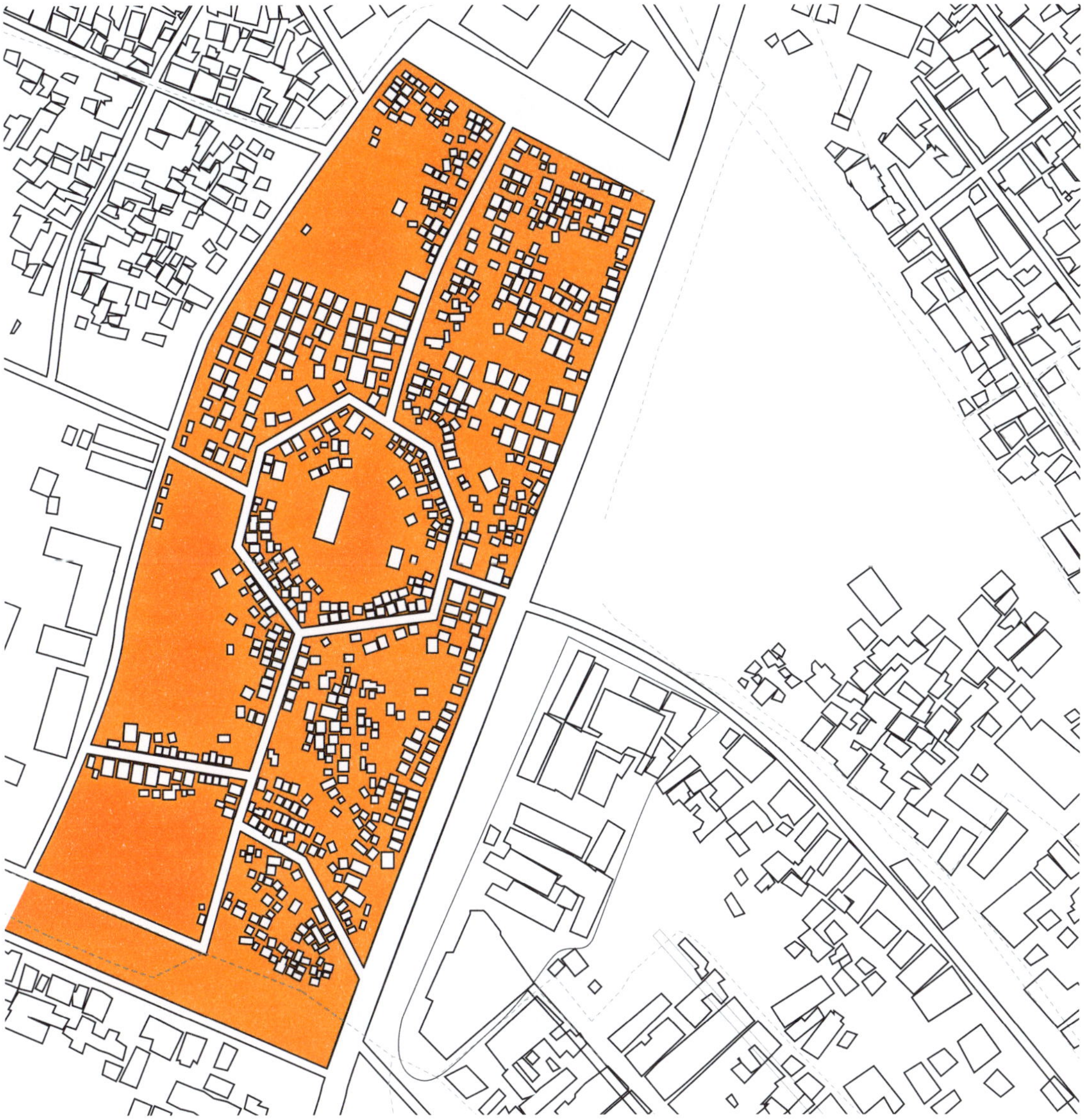

SONAPI

This industrial park is a tax-free export processing zone located between the international port and airport, close to two major slums which house most of the workers. While SONAPI is sited on state-owned land, its status as a free zone contributes to the effect of an urban island through its specialized laws and protections. It is guarded by MINUSTAH forces headquartered in Buildings 2 and 14.

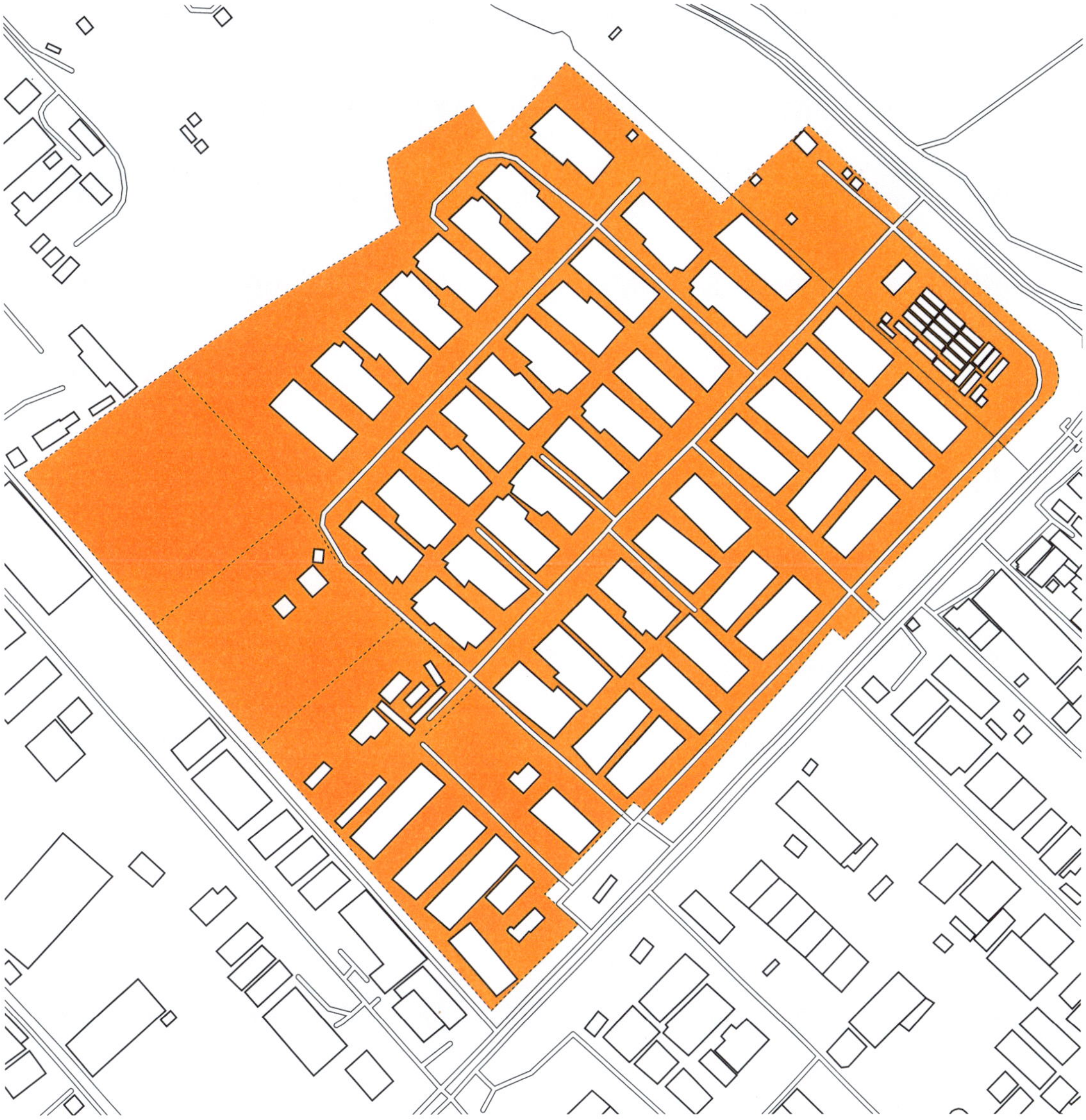

UNON Gigiri compound

The world headquarters of UN-Habitat and UNEP are located within a compound adjacent to a nature preserve on the outskirts of northern Nairobi. The compound receives the benefits of extraterritorial status, governed by international law and administered by the UN. The park houses the regional offices of numerous other UN groups, along with the local branches of the World Bank, World Food Programme, World Health Organization, and International Monetary Fund. The campus maintains a park-like atmosphere, including the Gigiri Nature Trail, preserving its separation from the city as a securitized island for diplomats and other rare species.

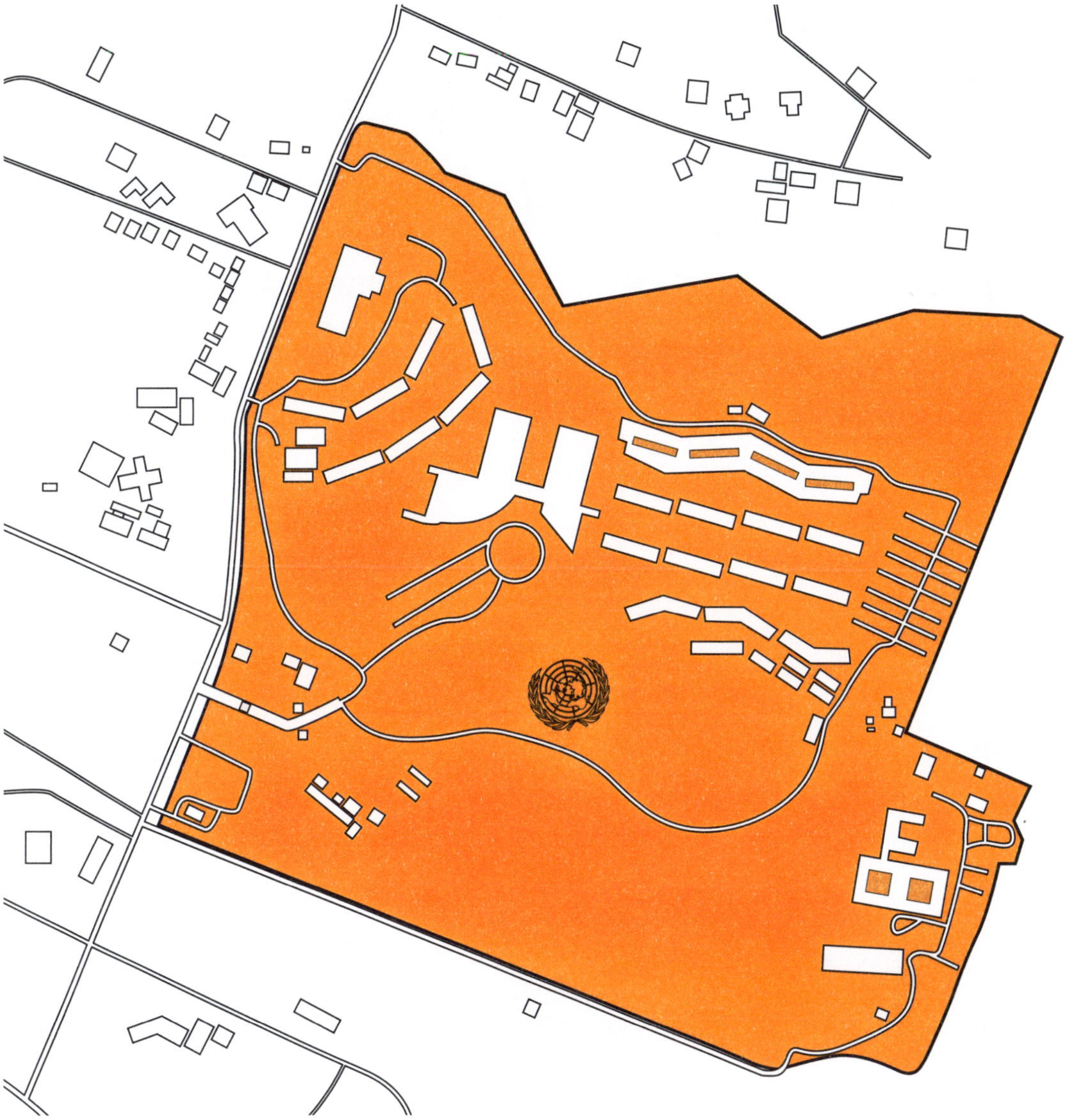

Mishor Adumim

The entirety of Ma'ale Adumim and Mishor Adumim were originally set aside by the Israeli government in 1967 as the site of a future industrial park. The industrial and residential areas grew together, each supporting the expansion of the other within the protected classification of their territory. While Ma'ale Adumim is now recognized as a municipality, Mishor Adumim retains its original status, and more than 300 businesses located there currently enjoy special tax benefits under Israeli law.

Kibera slum

Once the recognized territory of Kenya's Nubian community, Kibera was expropriated by the Kenyan government after independence in 1963 and designated a national forest. Residents who had previously been considered homeowners were declared "unauthorized settlers," and eventually Kibera became known as one of the largest slums in Africa. Its territory and number of inhabitants is highly disputed, with population estimates ranging from 170,070 to 2 million, and an area estimated between 120 to 1780 hectares. The slum retains the designation of national forest that it was given after independence, and though there are very few plants and fewer trees in Kibera, its status makes it at once geographically inside the city and outside its normal legal regime of property rights.

2. Port-au-Prince and Humanitarian Liberalism

In some cities, it seems possible to point to a singular moment of crisis, a brief period of acute violence or destruction that has permanently shaped the form of the city and its regional and international relationships. The effects of an isolated event—a natural disaster, an armed uprising, a famine, or military coup—are seen afterward in the shape of the city that results: the displacement and relocation of populations, the clearance of certain neighborhoods, or the redevelopment of an urban center following a war. The buildings of the city become a material record of a discrete eruption of violence that leaves a legible history in the structures inhabited by its residents. The presumed stability of architecture, even in a damaged or altered state, stands in for the restabilization of a city after the resolution of a crisis.

In Port-au-Prince, crisis is not an isolated or easily identifiable moment. While the earthquake of January 12, 2010, may appear as a singular event in the country's recent history, it is perhaps better understood within a longer continuum of violence in the city, with sites, actors, and organizations that take part in a slower, more durable conflict. Violence here is not simply military or gang-fueled, or even the environmental violence of a natural disaster, but rather assumes many modalities: economic liberalization, international investment, humanitarian aid, nongovernmental de facto governance, and more than a decade of peacekeeping operations. The city form, rather than registering a discrete moment of crisis, becomes elastic, expanding and contracting according to the pressures exerted upon it.

Haiti's earthquake in 2010 wrought more destruction than any other earthquake of its magnitude in history. In Port-au-Prince, the headquarters of the UN's peacekeeping mission collapsed. The marine port, Terminal Varreux, was heavily damaged and unable to receive shipments. Large portions of Toussaint Louverture International Airport caved in and commercial flights stopped. The Presidential Palace was destroyed. All of the city's hospitals were damaged. The phones lines went silent; the power went out. But the earthquake was less an event than an abrupt exacerbation of a slower-moving economic violence of development, peacekeeping operations, and humanitarian interventions over the previous decades.

Driving through Port-au-Prince a year after the earthquake with a friend who was raised in that city, she pointed from the car window and narrated to us which passing piles of rubble were the result of earthquake and which were a normal part of the streetscape. What looked to us like a row of recently collapsed houses had actually been a stalled construction site for twenty years; a road in terrible condition was really a slow-moving public works project; a house at the bottom of a ravine was not a victim of the earthquake, but had fallen in a mudslide after a rain storm, tumbling down the steep hill where those without the advantage of land tenure had built their homes. It was an eye-opening drive, realizing how much nuance was lost in the images of the city in the aftermath of the earthquake.

Seen this way, the earthquake was only one moment in a history of continual crisis. Understood through the built form of the city, crisis is a durable, even mundane condition, not an event. The indistinguishability of the disastrous and the mundane defined Port-au-Prince after the earthquake, a city that has existed in crisis for decades, living under occupation by foreign troops, with downtown neighborhoods so violent that they are compared to war zones even in peacetime. Rates of murder in the slum Cité Soleil from 2007 to 2013 were so high that the numbers of violent deaths in Haiti rivaled those of nations emerging from civil wars.[1] This was the same period in which the UN Stabilisation Mission to Haiti (MINUSTAH), a peacekeeping force that is regularly described as one of the UN's most successful, was charged with maintaining security in Port-au-Prince.

During the earthquake, the face of the hill on the right collapsed.

1 United Nations Office on Drugs and Crime, *Global Study on Homicide 2013: Trends, Context, Data* (2013), 19, goo.gl/V06Ka0.

The expansion and contraction of crisis is most visibly manifest in the proliferation and periodic demolition of unauthorized settlements, often called slums, around Port-au-Prince. These areas are not spontaneous excrescences nor even what is commonly called informal;[2] rather they exist as part of a distinct form integrating three coconstituted urban types—the slum, the zone, and the port—that comprise a surprisingly enduring infrastructure that links the labor market of the city to multinational companies and international institutions. In Port-au-Prince, as in many cities, these three types are found nearly adjacent to one another on the outskirts of the historic urban center. The relations between these three types describes the effects of humanitarian-military operations on Port-au-Prince in their capacity to integrate areas of the city into an international order: the slum (Cité Soleil), the free trade zone (the SONAPI and SHODECOSA export processing zones), and the ports (Terminal Varreux Marine Port and Toussaint Louverture International Airport). These sites are not singular spaces, but rather are exemplary of a larger infrastructure into which they are embedded, incorporating a range of actors and organizations in the humanitarian urbanism of Port-au-Prince.

2 "Informal," as it is used in this sense, refers to urban developments that are not legally or officially sanctioned. As we discuss in this chapter, Cité Soleil is not, strictly speaking, an informal settlement, since it began as a government housing project aligned with the creation of the nearby Export Processing Zone.

Each spatial type occupies a specific extralegal or extraterritorial position: the slums exist outside the system of land tenure and real property; the *zones d'attente* of the airport are legally international territory; and the industrial zone is designed to evade local taxes and regulatory frameworks. They are an inclusive exclusion in the city, as Giorgio Agamben might say, spatial types that act as loopholes in the law and are therefore both outside and integral to the order of the city.[3] The slum, the zone, and the port form a complex that short-circuits the presumed geographical and legal hierarchy, in which the city is contained within the nation and the nation participates in international relations, creating a disintermediated relationship between transnational actors and the local population of Port-au-Prince.

3 Giorgio Agamben, *Homo Sacer: Sovereign Power and Bare Life*, trans. Daniel Heller-Roazen (Stanford: Stanford University Press, 1998).

Within this situation, the UN holds a particular status as a supranational entity representing the imagined international community and its interests. For more than a decade, MINUSTAH has maintained a presence in Port-au-Prince. During this time, its operations in the city have shifted from a peacekeeping mission following the ouster of Haitian President Jean-Bertrand Aristide in 2004 to a military offensive during a period of violent conflict in the Cité Soleil slum, and then to a coordinator of humanitarian aid after the 2010 earthquake. During this intervention in Port-au-Prince, MINUSTAH's activities have shaped the city, particularly in Cité Soleil and the adjacent SONAPI Export Processing Zone (EPZ), a complex of factories, many serving the international garment industry, where MINUSTAH guards the gates and maintains an operational base.

MINUSTAH's mission in Port-au-Prince suggests the degree to which the field of international military operations has expanded beyond wars between nations to include the maintenance of international security through humanitarian-military interventions. The mandate for such a mission can be expansive and changing; the battalions of MINUSTAH exercise a power in the city that extends beyond the expected limits of a peacekeeping force, acting on behalf of economic interests, security imperatives, and humanitarian operations, both before and after the earthquake. The continuous low-level violence of the areas in which MINUSTAH operates is a product of a spatial short circuit, in which a part of a city is ruptured from the state-nation-territory trinity and ceded to multiple supranational entities with limited accountability to the populations they now administer. The operations of the international peacekeeping mission oscillate between armed warfare, humanitarian assistance, policing, security, and logistics in service of development aid, and ultimately the urban planning of the city.

In our conversations with the leader of Architecture for Humanity's postearthquake relief efforts in Haiti, Eric Cesal, he described the fundamental divergence he saw between aid organizations. As he explained to us then, Haiti after the earthquake was caught between two mentalities in the aid community: emergency management and developmentalism. The first approach dominates among the groups that distribute rice and tarps long after the immediate months following a disaster. It allows them to build in the city without concern for the longer-term implications, resulting in temporary shelters that are vulnerable to the rainy season and the hurricane season. It is a mind-set that prioritizes security, and it builds camps and sustains them indefinitely. In the aftermath of the 2010 earthquake, the humanitarian architecture that derives from this approach was highly visible in the city's sprawling tent camps, seen in the new temporary medical clinics and the schools housed in shipping containers donated by international NGOs. This approach results in an architecture that simultaneously declares both its own good intentions and the limits of its capacity to end poverty and suffering.

MINUSTAH troops guarding the entrance to the destroyed National Palace

The second mentality, developmentalism, views liberalization of local economies as the most promising path for delivering aid. Developmentalism results in a very different type of humanitarian architecture. Rather than directly and materially reproducing the camp and its temporary shelters, it invests in office buildings and factories, industrial parks and free trade zones. These buildings offer both economic and moral returns for those who give, and its forms are less easily discernible within the city. These are the buildings that hide in plain sight.

For decades, international trade policies supported by aid organizations have shaped the growth and development of Port-au-Prince, acting through policy and international development aid to construct the three forms (the slum, the zone, and the port) that define the city's urbanism. With the creation and deployment of MINUSTAH, there was a shift in scale, a refinement in the precision of actions from the national or urban scale to the scale of the neighborhood and building. Policy papers and aid programs that had fueled the growth of slums, built the zone, and expanded the port were replaced by a militarized international presence within all three spaces. These three forms are the result of humanitarian action; they are humanitarian spaces; they produce humanitarian subjects.

The Slums

Cité Soleil today is a dense and sprawling agglomeration of low buildings, often described as the poorest and most dangerous place in the Western hemisphere. Lacking formal land tenure and constructed with substandard building materials, the area has almost no access to water, sewer, or electrical infrastructure.[4] A favorite image of foreign journalists reporting from the slum is the scene of women producing "mud cakes"—dried platters of dirt, salt, and margarine eaten to stave off hunger when food is too unaffordable. But despite the image of Cité Soleil's corrugated metal roofs and open sewer trenches, the area is not, in contemporary parlance, an informal community.

4 Louis Herns Marcelin, "Cooperation, Peace, and (Re-)Construction? A Tale from the Shanties," *Journal of Peacebuilding & Development* 6, no. 3 (2011): 21. See also UN Habitat, *Strategic Citywide Spatial Planning: A Situational Analysis of Metropolitan Port-au-Prince, Haiti* (Nairobi: UN-Habitat, 2009).

Indeed, the history of Cité Soleil belies its current appearance. In 1958 the community was developed by the national government, under the name Cité Simone, with the construction of homes for fifty-two families as social housing under the presidency of François "Papa Doc" Duvalier (1957–71). Located outside the city boundaries at the time, between the airport and the harbor, Cité Simone was constructed on land that was previously owned by HASCO, a state-owned sugar production company, in the area of what is now the SONAPI EPZ. The relationship between worker housing and international trade has driven the development of Cité Soleil since its inception, as the families initially housed in Cité Simone were workers in the HASCO fields and factories.[5] Its site, on the highway connecting the airport and the harbor, contributed to its rise as the dominant source of low-wage labor for the manufacture and assembly of goods for international export.

5 USAID. *Project Paper Urban Health and Community Development—Phase II, 521-0159* (unpublished, May 1984), 1, goo.gl/ya4dvu.

The development of Cité Simone could be seen as part of the postwar tendency in urban planning toward model communities and new towns. It was a close contemporary of the early American planned communities, such as the Levittowns of the late 1950s and early 1960s, and it would not be until the early 1960s, with the planning of Reston, VA, that the era of the American postwar planned city (as opposed to suburb) is often considered to have begun.[6] On an urban scale, the construction of Cité Simone by the Duvalier government can be seen as an effort to present an image of Port-au-Prince as a modern city of industry. Named for the first lady at the time, Simone Duvalier, the community was explicitly connected through its name to the reputation of the American-backed regime, and was developed strategically by the young dictatorship, then only in its second year of power.

6 On American planned communities, including the Levittowns and Reston, see James Bailey, ed., *New Towns in America: The Design and Development Process* (London: Wiley, 1973).

Cité Simone's construction redrew the map of Port-au-Prince, eventually legally extending the city's municipal boundaries to the north to encompass its site.[7] In the subsequent decades, it continued to influence the shape of the city as well as areas beyond Port-au-Prince, acting as a major destination of rural-urban migration spurred by economic policies favoring low export tariffs under the Duvalier administrations. The rural poor who were drawn to it from the entire region, and whose self-built housing began to reshape and extend its boundaries, transformed the model village into a sprawling settlement. Throughout the 1980s and 1990s, the form of Cité Simone, renamed Cité Soleil after the coup against the Duvaliers in 1986, continued to shift and grow in direct response to the migration induced by the economic policies of the national government.[8]

7 Jean Maxius Bernard, *Participation et développement communautaire: Gestion de l'eau potable et organisation sociale à Cité Soleil* (Port-au-Prince: Collection Pensée Critique, 2012), 51.

8 Robert Muggah, "The Effects of Stabilization on Humanitarian Action in Haiti," *Disasters* 34, issue supplement S3 (2010): S451.

In the years following the first coup against President Jean-Bertrand Aristide in 1992, US-imposed trade sanctions on Haiti led to deteriorating conditions in Cité Soleil, as the demand for labor in the EPZ contracted. A simultaneous UN embargo limited goods entering the country to humanitarian food and medicine aid, further damaging industrial production and crippling the ability of local farmers to compete in the market for staple crops such as rice, which were distributed as food aid by USAID and other organizations.[9] The urbanization of Haitian poverty was fed by a massive migration from rural areas into the city during this period, driven by the sharp decline in the agricultural economy. The roots of this decline can be found in export policies and food aid packages which (intended or not) effectively reshaped rural and urban communities across the nation. The international trade policies initiated in the 1990s led to the decline of the rural agricultural economy which had supported the Haitian poor through economic downturns in the past, and increased the country's dependence on international aid.

9 Elizabeth Gibbons and Richard Garfield, "The Impact of Economic Sanctions on Health and Human Rights in Haiti, 1991–94," *American Journal of Public Health* 89, no. 10 (1999): 1499.

Even as it contributed to rising poverty rates and rapidly growing slums, urban overcrowding had its upsides for some. Massive unemployment and growing slum communities in downtown Port-au-Prince justified lower wages in the remaining industrial factories, especially in the garment industry, which was increasingly being kept afloat by economic policies introduced by the US Congress to give preferential treatment to US companies, presented as aid packages to Haiti.[10] Despite the pretense to altruism, aid and the urban consequences it engenders are not exempt from economic logic.

10 See HR 4889, the Haiti Economic Recovery Opportunity (HERO) Act, passed by the US Congress in 2004, goo.gl/Ejnv2a.

Aristide returned to power in 1994, but his second term was cut short by a coup in February 2004. Following the coup, an interim peacekeeping mission, the Multinational Interim Force (MIF) was authorized by the UN Security Council. It was soon replaced by MINUSTAH, which was formally established on June 1, 2004, by Security Council resolution 1542.

In the early years of the peacekeeping mission, Cité Soleil was a location of particular importance for MINUSTAH, as it was regarded as a stronghold of Aristide's party Fanmi Lavalas, as well as a site of frequent protests and an epicenter of gang activity, all of which contributed to the notion that Cité Soleil posed a threat to the city and nation.[11] Haitian gangs, while ostensibly criminal, perform a distinctly political function in areas like Cité Soleil. They are invoked by politicians as an implicit threat of violence during elections, and are also a source of resistance to both local government and international institutions.[12]

11 Walter Dorn, "Intelligence-Led Peacekeeping, The United Nations Stabilization Effort in Haiti (MINUSTAH), 2006–2007," *Intelligence and National Security* 24, no. 6 (2009): 812.

12 Michael Dziedzic and Robert M. Perito, *Confronting the Gangs of Port-au-Prince* (Washington, DC: US Institute for Peace, 2008), 2, goo.gl/29dT57.

Political conflicts notwithstanding, MINUSTAH also faced architectural challenges in their effort to stabilize and pacify the gangs of Cité Soleil. The dense and irregular configuration of buildings and the narrow footpaths which provided circulation made Cité Soleil an almost impenetrable space to MINUSTAH's battalions. The urban form of the slum was leveraged by residents as a kind of defensive space in resisting the military incursion by international peacekeepers. Like the revolutionary faubourgs during the Paris Commune, Cité Soleil's residents deployed the dense labyrinth of their neighborhood as a device to render their space illegible, unintelligible, and impenetrable by the peacekeepers.

MINUSTAH's first major operations to combat gangs in Cité Soleil took place in the Bois Neuf neighborhood on July 6, 2005, with the goal of capturing Emmanuel "Dread" Wilmé, variously described in coverage of the operation as a voodoo practitioner, gang boss, and community leader.[13] The July 6 operation killed Wilmé, but also resulted in the deaths of an unconfirmed number of civilians. Large protests occurred in the streets of Cité Soleil, followed by negative international press as activist groups accused the MINUSTAH forces of committing a massacre of civilians.[14]

13 Dorn, "Intelligence-Led Peacekeeping," 812 (see note 11).

14 As evidence of the attention given to this incident by activist organizations, see "Eyewitnesses Describe Massacre by UN Troops in Haitian Slum," *Democracy Now!* July 11, 2005, goo.gl/UrB5Yj; see also San Francisco Labor Council, "Growing Evidence of a Massacre by UN Occupation Forces in Port-au-Prince Neighborhood of Cité Soleil: Summary of Findings of the US Labor and Human Rights Delegation to Haiti," *Global Research*, July 14, 2005, goo.gl/XvRdjn.

Tensions between the Aristide-affiliated groups of Cité Soleil and the MINUSTAH forces came to a head during the winter of 2006.[15] Downtown Port-au-Prince had several major pro-Aristide protests in December 2006 through February 2007, some drawing thousands into the streets and raising the specter of partisan violence. In a political environment wherein the populist rhetoric of Aristide supporters was often conflated with high rates of gang violence, kidnappings, and murders—the unrest that MINUSTAH was charged with stabilizing—these rebellious bodies in the streets posed a direct threat to the UN effort.[16] MINUSTAH turned its attention back to Cité Soleil as a space through which conflict at a national level could be resolved by a relatively small-scale intervention. On December 22 a violent gun battle occurred between MINUSTAH and local groups in the Bois Neuf and Drouillard areas of Cité Soleil,[17] with at least nine confirmed casualties,[18] while Haitian activists and independent journalists estimated up to eighty deaths due to MINUSTAH gunfire.[19]

15 Reuters, "Surrender or Die, Haiti Tells Armed Gangs," *The Globe and Mail*, August 11, 2006, goo.gl/yPQcXY.

16 International Crisis Group, *Consolidating Stability in Haiti*, Latin America/Caribbean Report no. 21 (July 18, 2007), 11, goo.gl/B7aBGZ.

17 MINUSTAH press release 299, December 22, 2006, cited in International Crisis Group, *Consolidating Stability in Haiti*, 2 (see note 16).

18 "Monthly Forecast: Haiti," Security Council Report (February 2007), cited in International Crisis Group, *Consolidating Stability in Haiti*, 2 (see note 16).

19 Amy Goodman, interview with Kim Ives and Lovinsky Pierre-Antoine, "Another Massacre in Cité Soleil? Haitian Human Rights Activist Accuses UN of Killing Dozens in Recent Attach on Port-au-Prince Neighborhood," *Democracy Now*, December 29, 2006, goo.gl/sjuM6o.

In the immediate aftermath of the December 22 violence and the international attention which again followed the deaths of civilians at the hands of peacekeepers, the strategies of the MINUSTAH stabilization effort shifted from cycles of rapid incursion and retreat toward a more architecturally precise operation, through the capture and occupation of selected buildings within Cité Soleil. General Carlos Alberto dos Santos Cruz, the Brazilian commander who took over MINUSTAH in January 2007, implemented a systematic approach by first seizing strategic buildings around Cité Soleil and subsequently targeting the most high-profile gang leaders, while relying on MINUSTAH and HNP (Haitian National Police) intelligence to keep casualties as low as possible.[20] MINUSTAH's focus on the capture of specific buildings as an effort to stabilize the larger neighborhood was a militarized corollary to concurrent discussions of "urban acupuncture" and "tactical urbanism" within the fields of architecture and planning. When architects today advocate for tactical design strategies, it may bear recalling the origins of the metaphor of tactics: such techniques, as the term suggests, were developed first through military operations, as well as through violent resistance.

20 International Crisis Group, *Consolidating Stability in Haiti*, 2 (see note 16).

troops engaged in a "street cleaning effort" using not only brooms, but trucks and excavators, deploying the tools of large-scale infrastructure and public works operations in the service of "peacekeeping."[23]

22 Ibid.

23 Dorn, "Intelligence-Led Peacekeeping," 816 (see note 11).

A UN armored personnel carrier set on blocks and surrounded by barbed wire, creating a mobile tower.

As part of MINUSTAH's renewed approach to maintaining control through an armed presence within Cité Soleil under General Santos Cruz, checkpoints were created on key circulation routes and troops were deployed within the neighborhood, nominally with the goal of returning authority to the HNP after stabilizing the area and making it safe for government and aid workers to operate.[21] These checkpoints acted as gates to the community, modulating the flow of the population and exerting control over a large urban area through a network of key locations.

21 Ibid., 3.

The conflict between MINUSTAH troops and gangs in Cité Soleil was played out not only in the seizure of specific buildings, but also on the topographical surface of the streets themselves. In a gun battle between MINUSTAH and the followers of a local leader, Évens Jeune, who went by the name of "Ti Kouto" ("Little Knife"), in the Jamaica neighborhood of Cité Soleil, residents dug trenches through the streets to halt the passage of MINUSTAH vehicles, turning the streetscapes into a defensive structure, a kind of inverted barricade. In response, MINUSTAH filled the ditches with sand from the backs of trucks, rebuilding the road surface to create pathways for their operations, literally smoothing out the space of the battlefield.[22] To ensure continued secure access to the space of Cité Soleil, MINUSTAH

The challenge of entrance and visibility for MINUSTAH troops, as evidenced by the difficulty navigating narrow paths dug with trenches, was addressed through the Haussmann-style clearance of a portion of the slum and the construction of a small park in the center of Cité Soleil in 2008 with funding from USAID and the International Organization for Migration. In this case, aid funding was used directly for urban planning and construction intended to bolster MINUSTAH's ability to act on the immediate environment in the name of security. The park was created by clearing several dozen homes adjacent to Route Nationale 9, directly across from what became MINUSTAH's main headquarters in Cité Soleil. In a seemingly unconventional use of development aid, USAID gave a grant to the American defense contractor DynCorp to expand the MINUSTAH compound opposite the park, which resulted in the demolition of dozens of homes in 2009.[24] Rather than creating shelter or housing displaced people, as might be expected, aid money, in this case, was used to enlarge military operations while rendering families homeless.

24 Muggah, "The Effects of Stabilization on Humanitarian Action in Haiti," S452 (see note 8).

Indeed, the aims of MINUSTAH's humanitarian-military operations are not self-evidently aligned with the efforts of the various NGOs working in the neighborhood, and at times have come into direct conflict with them. On January 24, 2006, MINUSTAH troops seized control of a gang leader's headquarters, a four-story building known locally as "the Blue House," which was adjacent to a water tower that served as a source of clean drinking water for local residents near the entrance to the Boston sector. The water tower had been developed as a cooperative effort between multiple international aid organizations, including USAID, the International Organization for Migration, the International Committee of the Red Cross (ICRC), and the Haitian drinking water agency CAMEP (Centrale Autonome Métropolitaine d'Eau Potable). When MINUSTAH forces seized the Blue House, they posted guards on the scaffolding of the water tower, which had already been damaged in the gunfire during the siege of the building. CAMEP raised concerns that the troops' presence would make the tower a target for violence. MINUSTAH withdrew their troops from the water tower, and, according to the International Crisis group, building damages were repaired and the water source returned to full functionality.[25]

25 International Crisis Group, *Consolidating Stability in Haiti*, 2, 12 (see note 16).

Houses in Port-au-Prince destroyed by the earthquake

That the same building had been an operational space for gang leaders, MINUSTAH, and a group of international NGOs is no coincidence. All of the groups using the Blue House as a base of operations were guided by a similar spatial analysis of Cité Soleil. The Blue House was located at a key crossroads leading into a poor neighborhood (the area of Cité Soleil known as Boston) with little to no access to infrastructure or sanitation, which made the building attractive to both the humanitarians wishing to bring peace through clean water and to the military stabilization effort, which viewed the neighborhood's large and disenfranchised population as a political tinderbox threatening national stability. While MINUSTAH and the aid organizations drew similar conclusions about the spatial significance of the site, their divergent operational mandates led to separate approaches to the reuse, transformation, and redeployment of the simple building. The Blue House was seen by both groups as a step toward stabilization and economic integration, a stated goal shared by both MINUSTAH and the aid agencies. Whether dispensing gunfire or drinking water, the building was a carefully manipulated instrument of the stabilization effort within the neighborhood and the nation.

The Blue House is one of several homes and headquarters of local leaders that were seized and occupied by MINUSTAH troops during the course of their operations in Cité Soleil. MINUSTAH's presence transformed the buildings from sites of political resistance into bases for armed international peacekeeping efforts and surveillance of the surrounding buildings. Évens Ti Kouto's former headquarters at Jamaica Base, which had served as a residence, community gathering point, and arsenal, now houses a free medical clinic and provides a large public square for public performances, where the backdrop for the stage is the blue UN logo.[26]

26 United Nations News Centre, "Haiti: UN Peacekeepers Arrest Gang Chief in Ongoing Anti-Crime Blitz," February 20, 2007, goo.gl/GNCZRb.

Checkpoints, fortified streets, dense neighborhoods cleared for parks, houses turned to bunkers and surveillance towers: each of these architectural strategies was used by MINUSTAH in Cité Soleil to project and maintain control over the neighborhood. With varying intensities of violence, these spaces in Cité Soleil acted as power projection platforms (to borrow a term from the military lexicon), which kept the area both central to and excluded from the larger city. In pacifying the neighborhood, MINUSTAH produced humanitarian subjects out of its residents, turning citizens who had once resisted national and foreign military power into recipients of aid.

In the aftermath of the earthquake, the changing circumstances forced MINUSTAH into a new role in Cité Soleil, a hybrid between a police force and disaster relief logistics coordinator. The earthquake crippled the Haitian government's already tenuous ability to police and adminster the city by killing more than a third of the nation's civil servants, destroying the National Palace, and rupturing the walls of a national prison, allowing prisoners to escape into the streets of the capital.[27]

27 J. C. Gaillard and Fanny Navizet, "Prisons, Prisoners, and Disaster," *International Journal of Disaster Risk Reduction* 1 (2012): 34.

In the dust and rubble of the earthquake's aftermath, certain patterns of building survival emerged. Lightweight and flexible materials had fared better, for example; the elasticity of wooden frame buildings absorbed the shockwaves of the earthquake. In Port-au-Prince, buildings of this type tend to be concentrated in the poorer neighborhoods, the dense slums, and the squatted hillside communities where the majority of housing stock is self-built and constructed of temporary materials. Wood, metal sheeting, bamboo, wattle-and-daub—all the visual cues of poverty ironically may have saved many of the nation's poorest.

In Cité Soleil, the material qualities of the buildings were able to temper the loss of life during the earthquake. The preponderance of lightweight building materials such as corrugated sheet metal and thin wood structures meant that individual homes were more flexible than the middle-class houses in other neighborhoods built of concrete masonry, and were also less likely to crush residents in case of collapse. But the density of the housing stock meant that when one building fell, it was also likely to cause serious damage to the buildings adjacent to its walls, a domino effect resulting in swaths of flattened structures.[28] Whereas other parts of the city suffered damage largely in direct relationship to the quality of materials in an individual dwelling unit, in Cité Soleil the urban form itself was destructive.

28 Kathleen A. Tobin, "Population Density and Housing in Port-au-Prince: Historical Construction of Vulnerability," *Journal of Urban History* 39, no. 6 (2013): 1053–54.

The material construction of Cité Soleil is not an accident of urban development, but a physical manifestation of economic and military violence applied over decades. While the organization of the slum appears informal and spontaneous, its formal and material qualities have been dictated by the exercise of power at multiple scales, resulting in a legible order that is replicated around the world. Specifically, this order is tied to the integration of Haiti into the global economy, as the area receives a regular influx of rural migrants to provide the surplus labor that keeps Haiti a low-cost leader in the Western hemisphere for export production.

After the earthquake, Place la Fierté, the park that the UN had created in Cité Soleil by bulldozing the self-built houses of many families across from the headquarters of the Brazilian MINUSTAH battalion, was once again filled with spontaneous construction. With the construction of the IDP camp, the park was pressed into humanitarian operation, both to shelter survivors and as an aid and food distribution point. This single space was transformed through a decade of aid operations from a residential slum area into a militarized park, then into a camp and an aid distribution point, through each phase exerting a different form of power on the surrounding community.

The Zones

In 1969, less than ten years after the first houses were built in Cité Soleil, the first generation of US-based international export operations appeared in Haiti under François Duvalier, culminating in 1969 with the formation of SONAPI, the Société Nationale des Parcs Industriels, the national government's bureau managing the country's tax-free industrial zones.[29] Its first project was the construction of the Parc Industriel Métropolitaine in Port-au-Prince near Cité Soleil, an EPZ that is locally referred to as SONAPI, taking the name of its parent organization.

29 Jean-Germain Gros, "Anatomy of a Haitian Tragedy: When the Fury of Nature Meets the Debility of the State," *Journal of Black Studies* 42, no. 2 (2011): 141.

The initial investment by US companies was followed by a second wave in the 1970s and early 1980s when Papa Doc's son, Jean-Claude "Baby Doc" Duvalier, aggressively promoted the export-assembly industry to international investors.[30] Enabled by national and international trade incentives, additional EPZs were created near the city center and sited close to the shipping port and airport, generating strong demand for low-wage workers and access to export infrastructure.[31]

30 Francois Pierre-Louis, "Earthquakes, Nongovernmental Organizations, and Governance in Haiti," *Journal of Black Studies* 42, no. 2 (2011): 193.

31 Yasmine Shamsie, "Time for a 'High-Road' Approach to EPZ Development in Haiti," paper presented at the Social Science Research Council: Conflict Prevention and Peace Forum, January 24, 2011, goo.gl/z4SfCE.

The industrial zones exerted an influence beyond the immediate context of the city as well. Even poorly paid jobs in the growing manufacturing industry represented an attractive opportunity for Haitians in the rural mountain areas to leave subsistence farming for industrial work. Arriving workers settled in the low-lying floodplain of Port-au-Prince, resulting in a dramatic increase in housing costs in that area.[32] Cité Soleil drew new arrivals into its peripheral relationship to the city and its land tenure system, and the opportunity to live in low-cost or self-built housing within the slum while seeking employment in the EPZ, within walking distance of the workers' homes.[33]

32 Yasmine Shamsie, "Export Processing Zones: The Purported Glimmer in Haiti's Development Murk," *Review of International Political Economy* 16, no. 4 (2009): 657.

33 Jean Carmalt, "Prioritizing Health: A Human Rights Analysis of Disaster, Vulnerability, and Urbanization in New Orleans and Port-au-Prince," *Health and Human Rights* 16, no. 1 (2014): 48.

The development plan carried out by the consecutive Duvalier dictatorships and backed by international institutions between the 1960s and 1980s entailed a two-pronged approach toward an export-based economy. During the same period (1975–85) that export-assembly manufacturing reached its peak in investment and jobs, the urban industrial model developed its parallel in rural communities, where new agroindustrial export policies effectively shifted one-third of all cultivable land away from diverse landscapes of food production for subsistence and local trade toward a monoculture of export crops to be shipped from the same airport and harbor used by the new manufacturing facilities.[34]

34 Shamsie, "Export Processing Zones," 656 (see note 32).

The late 1980s were a turning point for the agricultural and industrial sectors in Haiti, in establishing a network of relations between workers migrating from the hills to the slums, the formation of EPZs, and the flow of goods and money through the airport and harbor that continues to shape Port-au-Prince today. Under the Duvalier presidencies, Haiti had resisted demands to lower the 50 percent tariff on imported foods, protecting the national agricultural sector as well as rural subsistence farmers and their traditional way of life. After Baby Doc was ousted by the military in February 1986, the United States successfully lobbied the interim government of General Henri Namphy to liberalize the Haitian economy by ending subsidies to farmers and dramatically reducing tariffs on imported goods.[35] USAID declared in a report that "deeper market interdependence with the United States [would] provide the preconditions for Haiti to become the 'Taiwan of the Caribbean.'"[36] International assembly firms located in the EPZs at the center of Port-au-Prince were crucial to this integrated rural-urban development strategy, as the industry was expected to absorb the labor of the rural population displaced as a result of the shift from subsistence agriculture to agricultural export production. The dual approach to economic integration in Haiti pulled hundreds of thousands into Port-au-Prince, many of them to Cité Soleil.[37] In the late 1980s, under the interim presidency of General Namphy, Haitian economist and finance minister Leslie Delatour advocated for the further depopulation of much of the Haitian countryside, and the relocation of those populations to sites such as Cité Soleil where workers could be employed in the new factories. Under Minister Delatour, the state closed down HASCO in 1987, and the last major agricultural employer in the metropolitan region was gone.[38]

35 Alex Dupuy, "Class, Power, Sovereignty: Haiti Before and After the Earthquake," in *Caribbean Sovereignty, Development and Democracy in an Age of Globalization*, ed. Linden Lewis (New York: Routledge, 2013), 23.

36 Carmen Diana Deere and Peggy Antrobus, eds., *In the Shadow of the Sun: Caribbean Development Alternatives and U.S. Policy* (Boulder: Westview Press, 1990), 175.

37 Tobin, "Population Density and Housing in Port-au-Prince," 1053–54 (see note 28).

38 Mats Lundahl, *Politics or Markets? Essays on Haitian Underdevelopment* (London: Routledge, 1992), 91–95.

By the early 1980s, Port-au-Prince was home to more than 240 multinational corporations, employing between 40,000 and 60,000 workers (mostly women) at the lowest wages in the hemisphere.[39] Yet even at the height of its productivity, the assembly industry never employed more than 7 percent of Port-au-Prince's workforce, in comparison with the conservative estimates of 38 percent urban workforce unemployment at the time. In 1985, one year prior to the end of Baby Doc's rule, more than half Haiti's industrial exports went to the US and yet earned only one-quarter of the country's foreign exchange, due to the preferential trade agreements with American companies.[40] The city was shaped by these policies both politically and spatially as the dictatorship of the US-backed Duvalier family neared its close. Port-au-Prince had a population of 150,000 in 1950, 732,000 in the early 1980s, and 3 million in 2008, approximately one-third of the country's total population in a city designed for 200,000 people. The construction of SONAPI, a walled export zone, today guarded by a joint team of MINUSTAH troops and HNP forces, contributed to the overpopulation of the city at the time of the earthquake.

39 Shamsie, "Export Processing Zones," 657 (see note 32).

40 Ibid., 657.

SONAPI is only one site in a network of EPZs, including SHODECOSA in Port-au-Prince and the Caracol EPZ in the north of Haiti. On SHODECOSA's website, the EPZ is described as "Haiti's 'bread basket' because of its use as a long-term humanitarian food storage facility by internationally renowned agencies" including USAID, ACDI, the Red Cross, and the World Food Programme, among others. SHODECOSA, like SONAPI, is located next to Cité Soleil, and is also adjacent to the marine port, Terminal Varreux. Both SHODECOSA and the port are owned by the Mevs family, a business dynasty in Port-au-Prince, through which large quantities of import and export goods pass.

The day after Aristide departed Haiti in 2004, 4,500 American-led troops arrived in Port-au-Prince. The interim government which followed specifically promoted privatization and further movement to an export-based economy through a process called the Cadre de Coopération Intérimaire (CCI), a nominally cooperative effort between the Haitian government and foreign organizations which many Haitians nonetheless perceived as a violation of the country's sovereignty.

Legislation benefiting Haitian EPZs had been in progress in the US Congress prior to Aristide's departure, but gained momentum in its aftermath. The drafting of the Haitian Economic Recovery Opportunity Act (HERO) began in 2003, but was only passed in July 2004 after Aristide's departure, and just days before the CCI framework was ratified in Washington. The legislation was reintroduced as the Haiti Hemispheric Opportunity through Partnership Encouragement Act (HOPE) in 2006, and was passed again. The HERO and HOPE acts extended free trade privileges and tax exemption to textile factory owners, the majority of whom were based in the US, who drew their workforces from slums such as Cité Soleil, and operated from within EPZs like SONAPI. The physical space of the EPZs acts as an apparatus to instantiate political decisions and economic agreements within a particular, localized place and living routines, connecting acts of legislation to the physical spaces of the city.

After the 2010 earthquake, the EPZs were used by a number of relief organizations as emergency logistics bases and warehouses for food. Riding the wave of international money that was pledged for the rebuilding effort, a program and facility called the Haiti Apparel Center (HAC) was constructed at the SONAPI EPZ. An approximately 560-square-meter garment factory, the HAC benefits from USAID funding and the operational support of groups including the relief organization CHF International. It offers a garment worker training program intended to produce a more skilled workforce, supposedly for the advancement of the workers, but benefitting the textile export manufacturers at least as much. Billed as job training, the program includes a six-to-eight-week unpaid training period with a curriculum written by a garment industry buyers' association and has no guarantee of employment at completion.[41]

41 Information about the Haiti Apparel Center based on a visit by the authors and interviews with managers of the facility in June 2010.

The entrance to the SONAPI EPZ is guarded by UN MINUSTAH forces.

In early summer 2010 we toured the HAC and its surrounding factories with the manager of the project, a Haitian named Michel Pun. He was gracious and generous in his explanations of the HAC and seemed fully convinced of its positive value to the business community of Port-au-Prince. We visited the site just after construction had been completed and only one week prior to commencement of classes for the garment workers. In this brief period when the construction work was complete and before its operations began, the unoccupied building had a preternaturally pristine quality, its long-span structure hovering over the shiny new Juki sewing machines with billowing dust covers. Mr. Pun estimated the cost of the single-story steel-frame facility to be just over a million dollars and enthusiastically described how he could readily replicate the building with more funding from international donors. The money for this project was given by the Clinton Global Initiative, the Juki Corporation, CHF, and others; the owners and operators of the HAC are also the owners of the surrounding factories.

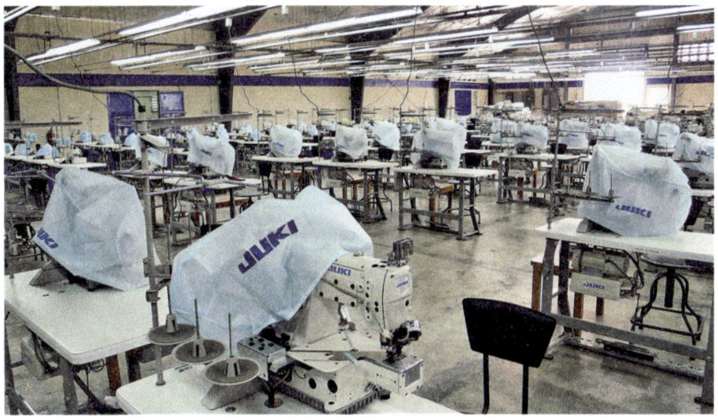

Inside the Haiti Apparel Center in SONAPI, funded by USAID, the Clinton Global Initiative, CHF, and the Juki Corporation

The HAC's training courses have the effect of significantly lowering the costs to factory owners of training new employees to use the sewing machines and factory equipment more efficiently. As Michel Pun explained to us during our tour of the facilities, a newly hired employee is not as profitable to the owners during the first three months of their job, when they are still being trained but are already earning a paycheck. The HAC aims to increase those early profits to the companies—foreign corporations renting space in a walled and militarized industrial zone—by replacing the less profitable salaried training period for employees with unpaid training for aspiring job applicants. The completion of these training courses does not guarantee employment in the SONAPI factories nor do graduates necessarily command higher wages for their skills. The greatest value of this humanitarian building is in the increased profit margins of foreign-owned export companies with histories of labor abuses and violations. The factory owners are an unusual, perhaps surprising, class of humanitarian subjects, the recipients of aid in the form of a large training facility for their businesses.

In an August 11, 2010, press release, USAID touted the proximity of the HAC to Cité Soleil, writing that the facility in the EPZ was located "minutes from the garment factories in and around Port-au-Prince and close to workers' residential neighborhoods."[42] The EPZ and Cité Soleil are part of a common apparatus, a system of biopolitical control promoting economic integration with low barriers to trade, low wages, no land tenure, and no job security or wage protection. The EPZ is a space where intangible trade policies are physicalized in a site, and suspect labor practices masquerade as humanitarian aid. While the factories in SONAPI have been called sweatshops by labor-rights groups, the term, in referring to a specific building form, does not begin to capture the larger set of relations that is animated by the facilities in SONAPI. Condemning an individual sweatshop distracts from the larger structures that built it in the first place, and the ongoing work required to maintain its operations. It is perhaps more useful to consider the building as part of a much larger apparatus, a point where globalized labor and trade policies intersect with humanitarian aid. Such large-scale buildings and operations require the engagement of many parties, from traditional humanitarian aid groups to corporate investors, contractors, and military personnel. SONAPI, for example, is a point of confluence of economic, political, and military power; in addition to housing the export processing zone, it has been used as a polling place for UN-sponsored elections after Aristide's ouster, and as a base for MINUSTAH.

42 USAID Press Office, "New USAID-Funded Haiti Apparel Center to Provide Training to Thousands of Haitians in the Garment Industry," August 11, 2010, goo.gl/ngpnVl.

The aggregation of varied interests, needs, and approaches in Haiti after the 2010 earthquake produced incredibly nuanced and complex forms of humanitarian architecture. The EPZs have become multifarious sites of humanitarian management, serving as an operational base of humanitarian relief and postearthquake logistics, a channel for development aid in exchange for economic integration with the United States, a platform for military operations beyond its walls, and even as a civic institution. Most importantly, they are nodes in the infrastructural network of export processing for the goods that leave the country through another integral site, the ports.

The Ports

The locations of the SONAPI and SHODECOSA EPZs were chosen in part for their proximity to the marine port and the airport. Together, the three spatial forms—the slum (labor), the zones (production), and the ports (distribution)—comprise a spatial-architectural mechanism by which value can be extracted from Haiti's labor force. The ports provide the means of circulating the physical materials that are part of the alchemy of the EPZ, by which a legal and financial arrangement is made operational through assumption of physical form. The ports are an interface between Haiti and international investors, acting as a gateway for the material resources required for processing and the commodities subsequently produced for export.

The rebuilding of the historic Iron Market after the earthquake

Most of the materials used in the export production industries pass through Terminal Varreux, the main commercial port of Port-au-Prince. Terminal Varreux was built in the 1970s by the Mevs family, a Haitian industrial dynasty. The port is still owned by their company, the WIN Group, a century-old conglomerate that was instrumental in the planning and construction of SHODECOSA and Cité Simone, and also retains a financial stake in SONAPI. Through their involvement in the EPZs, the WIN Group also maintains a tax-free area of the port that is not subject to government auditing. The company also operates SONTRAM (Société Nationale des Transports Maritimes), which provides the services and security for the marine port, and WINECO, which controls the importation of petroleum and natural gas through the ports.

The rebuilding efforts of the international community in Haiti have produced some rather unexpected bedfellows. In 2010 the WIN Group partnered with the Clinton Foundation, Architecture for Humanity, Habitat for Humanity, and the Soros Foundation to form the "North Pole Alliance," a group dedicated to creating another industrial hub for export processing north of Port-au-Prince. Though politics and economic policies have brought these groups together in Port-au-Prince, their mutual interests in many ways prefigure their meeting in Haiti. While Architecture for Humanity and Habitat for Humanity are the only organizations in the North Pole Alliance that are explicitly engaged in building construction as a humanitarian mission, other member groups work with architecture and urban planning in subtler ways, as a means to achieve or facilitate development aid and relief efforts.

The Clinton Foundation and the Soros Foundation each regularly fund rebuilding projects in Haiti. The Clinton Foundation in particular has prioritized design intervention as a means of humanitarian aid. Aside from their substantial financial contributions to the construction of the HAC and numerous grants made to smaller organizations providing temporary shelters, the Clinton Foundation has also sought to attach its name to the construction or reconstruction of several prominent buildings in the city. The renovation of the Iron Market in downtown Port-au-Prince was heavily funded by the Clinton Foundation and designed by an architecture firm, John McAslan Architects, with an extensive history working with the foundation in other contexts. Their selection of urban projects has been strategic, emphasizing buildings that can act as economic catalysts in the city and thereby align with the foundation's agenda of promoting development and integration into global markets. It is perhaps worth remembering that as president, Bill Clinton pressed Aristide to maintain low wages at SONAPI and promoted Haiti's integration into the Free Trade Alliance of the Americas.

The project of the North Pole Alliance, dubbed the West Indies Free Zone (WIFZ) was conceived in 2009, but after the earthquake it was reframed as development aid, with the partnership of the NGOs and foundations.[43] The WIFZ was slated for construction on a site adjacent to another project sponsored by the Clinton Foundation, the Haitian Government's Housing Expo, a model community with a variety of housing types contributed by international developers which grew out of the Clinton Foundation's Building Back Better Communities (BBBC) design competition. Residents of the Housing Expo model community in Zoranje, Haiti, were expected to form the labor resources of the WIFZ, and the WIFZ was intended to provide economic support to that model community in the form of factory employment. Both the Housing Expo and the WIFZ were cancelled in the summer of 2012.

43 "Haiti-based WIN Group and Soros Economic Development Fund Announce a $ 45 Million Commercial Zone in Haiti," *Business Wire*, October 6, 2009, goo.gl/yg5lj7.

In many ways these coupled designs of a free-trade zone and new housing development shared similarities with the rhetoric and spatial arrangement of Cité Simone and SONAPI during the 1950s and 60s. The groups developing the schemes (international aid groups planning the WIFZ, Haitian government and international aid groups planning the BBBC) promoted the zone and model community as an engine for an economic future driven by exports produced for the global marketplace. The WIN Group's cooperation with major charitable foundations on the West Indies Free Zone and the accompanying housing project is emblematic of the overlap between international development and humanitarian aid, and between corporations and non-governmental organizations. The marine terminals run by the WIN Group are both a channel for aid and for the goods that Haiti exports.

As the major logistical provider for Port-au-Prince, the WIN Group is both a beneficiary of humanitarian aid and a powerful agent of its control and distribution via its network of ports, factories, and warehouses. In addition to supplying raw materials for the EPZs and shipping their products, Terminal Varreux is also the transfer point for most of the food aid that Haiti receives, which is stored in the nearby SHODECOSA EPZ, in several warehouses leased by the World Food Programme. WIN also owns the smaller Terminal Gonaïves, making the company the channel for nearly all the humanitarian aid that entered Port-au-Prince following the earthquake.

In addition, two cruise ships, the *Sea Voyager* and the *Ola Esmeralda*, were docked for months at Terminal Varreux as accommodations for UN staff and relief workers, at a cost of $112,500 per day.[44] The cruise ships replicated the spatial logic of Haiti's tourist industry during its boom years of the 1970s: the "garrison tourism" of beachfront enclaves, where the security and comfort of the foreign visitors was maintained by separating them from the city.[45] Whether carrying tourists or UN staff, cruise ships maintain a self-sufficient environment constructed to the standards of the home country, one that is mobile and therefore presumably able to withdraw if the need arises.

44 "Haïti: Loin du stress des camps de réfugiés, les hôtels flottants de l'ONU," *Agence France Presse*, April 1, 2010, goo.gl/hjsANx. See also the World Food Programme's story about the arrival of the cruise ships: "WFP Shipping Brings Life to Haiti's Once Devastated Port-au-Prince Port," March 19, 2010, goo.gl/bz8NW7.

45 Stephen Graham, *Cities Under Siege: The New Military Urbanism* (London: Verso, 2010), 101.

Port-au-Prince's airports are also critical sites in the infrastructure of aid. MINUSTAH maintains a presence at Toussaint Louverture International Airport, where a separate area of the facility has been designated for the UN's use as the MINUSTAH Logistics Center since 2005. After the earthquake, the airport took on a greater significance and vastly heavier use as a humanitarian space with the influx of international aid organizations. The single runway of the airport handled more than 1,000 flights in the first week following the earthquake. The combination of debilitated government institutions, damage to the airport, and the increase in arriving flights led the Haitian government to request that the US military assume temporary custody of the airport following the earthquake, as they were perceived to be better able to manage the movement of air traffic into the city.[46] A US Air Force special operations team took control of the airport the day after the earthquake, less than half an hour after landing. Within a week, some amount of control had been returned to the Haitian government with the creation of the Haiti Flight Operations Coordination Center, which controlled landing times as set "by the Government of Haiti in consultation with the United States."[47] This seemingly innocuous administrative detail suggests the logistical value of the airport to the international aid effort after the earthquake. Toussaint Louverture Airport is not only a point of contact with the international community (which could be said of any international airport) but, like many of Haiti's institutions and infrastructures, it has an uncommon degree of direct foreign administration. The US involvement in the airport is not a recent phenomenon as funding for the airport came from grants given by the US during the prodevelopment administration of François Duvalier, for whom it was originally named.

46 Gros, "Anatomy of a Haitian Tragedy," 149 (see note 29).

47 Paul Koring, "A Once Sleepy Airport Is Now Haiti's Overstretched Lifeline," *The Globe and Mail*, January 19, 2010, goo.gl/uGqbTd.

In the early weeks after the 2010 earthquake a "Humanitarian Cargo Village" was created within the airport, with tents and prefabricated units erected to provide space for the ICRC, Médicins Sans Frontières, and other NGOS to coordinate logistical movements of supplies, fuel, and medicine.[48] Several years later, that area of the airport continues to be dedicated to humanitarian logistics, demonstrating that aid efforts, often begun in dramatic, fast-paced circumstances, may nonetheless produce durable spatial effects. The airport and marine port have become switch points in the circulation of goods and people arriving in and leaving Haiti, an interface between the international organizations and the local population. The ports are multifarious in their purposes, supporting the supply chain of aid, the movement of tax-free goods produced in the EPZs, and the staging of military-peacekeeping operations, acting as a conduit for the various kinds of traffic that move between Haiti and the rest of the world.

48 "Haiti: WFP Logistics POI," compiled by the WFP Emergency Preparedness and Response Branch (ODEP), February 7, 2010, goo.gl/9V1kMf.

Camps

Flying into Port-au-Prince in the spring 2010, the city appeared to be in the midst of a strange inversion. Neighborhoods had been reorganized, restructured; once densely inhabited blocks had been emptied and their residents dumped into the streets. This involution of the urban block produced a new image of the city seen from above, where a single form, the tent camp, dominated the landscape.

For most residents of first-world nations, the mediatized image of the camp stands in for its physical presence. If all that you knew of Port-au-Prince in early 2010 was received through the images circulated by television news, you could be forgiven for imagining that there were no other buildings left in the city, for assuming that the entire city had been replaced by tarp enclosures swaying and shuddering in the breeze. Major-channel news anchors placed themselves with the backdrop of these camps as symbols of the humanitarian crisis, demonstrations of both the human suffering and the outpouring of relief efforts. The tent camps became a green screen onto which the media and its viewers could project their assumptions about the disaster and its aftermath.

A tent camp in Port-au-Prince

Images of the city transmitted in the weeks after the 2010 earthquake foregrounded the various shacks, domes, shelters, and tarps distributed by some of the estimated 10,000 NGO groups working in Haiti.[49] Reporters and camera crews, many of whom arrived even before the aid workers, filmed their news segments in the open air of the streets of Port-au-Prince. The president of the Pew Research Center, Andrew Kohut, remarked in conversation with the *New York Times* on the media coverage of the 2010 earthquake, "This is a picture story, to a very large degree."[50] In an era of ever faster news cycles, the mediatized repetition of tent camp imagery created an iconographic relationship between the tent camp and the disaster. The identification between the crisis and the camps was reinforced through spatial and temporal repetition, with the camps sprawling across the city and their images looping in the news broadcasts.

49 Clinton Foundation press release, March 8, 2010, goo.gl/DuVy4P.

50 Brian Stelter, "Next News from Haiti: Pulling Out," *New York Times*, January 24, 2010, goo.gl/ZAm9Yg.

From the ground, the structures of relief aid were less visually constant but more disruptive to the routes and routines of the city. Movement was interrupted by camps that sprawled over roads, creating blockades or unexpected dead ends. Camps filled in any available open space in the city, from parks to golf courses to sidewalks, as well as the grounds of many private residences, factories, and office buildings. Temporary homes composited from tarps, scrap metal, and two-by-fours were built on the semicollapsed roofs, in the backyards, or in the street in front of houses that were destroyed in the earthquake, often as close as possible to the residents' former homes.

A tent camp in a park, across from the collapsed National Palace.

Walking through the streets, it seemed as if the city had been turned inside out, that the houses had suddenly and violently poured all of their inhabitants and some of their belongings into the streets. The dense sturdiness of concrete block could no longer be trusted; even those buildings not marked as condemned with spray paint were left vacant, guarded by their owners as they sat heavily in various states of collapse. The security of residences surrounded by tall walls topped with broken glass was replaced by the vulnerability of tarps: mobile, ubiquitous, repurposed for every need. Familiar landmarks had fallen; new ones proliferated.

Parks

In the months following the earthquake, there were no parks left in Port-au-Prince which had not been filled with tent camps. As a spatial type, parks have always functioned to provide a means for the city to incorporate an order outside itself. Previously in Port-au-Prince this other order was nature; following the earthquake, the camps replaced nature as the alien life in the city. The once-green open spaces in the city were transformed through their occupation by thousands of displaced families. This drastic restructuring of the public use of public land created an entirely new form of urban park, integrating and externalizing humanitarian space and subjectivity within the city.

There are other forms of park that are also exceptions to the normal order of the city: the industrial parks of the export processing zones, tariff-free manufacturing and logistical sites that are the points of interface between multinational corporations and the reserve army of Haiti's workforce. The EPZs are touted by the World Bank and others as benevolent agents of economic recovery and long-term development, and as an alignment of capital with humanitarian goals. Investment in the current EPZs, as well as development of new zones, has been a key piece of the proposals following both the political crisis of 2004 and the earthquake.[51]

51 The modernization of downtown Port-au-Prince via the development of large-scale workers' housing and the centralized export processing zone had far-reaching and long-lasting ramifications. Increased dependence on the foreign companies operating in the export processing zone sped the transition from an agriculture-based economy to one based in manufacturing and export. The ready availability of a low-cost, nonunionized workforce in Cité Soleil encouraged the development of an industrial manufacturing zone centered around the community. As technology advanced and the pace of global industry accelerated, urban planning reacted to these forces. The international airport was sited within easy reach of the export processing zone, forming a downtown nexus of interrelated sites devoted to low-cost manufacturing and export. Following the UN-led embargo of 1992–94, employment in the export processing zone decreased from 70,000 to 20,000, cutting off a major source of income to Cité Soleil. After this point, the transition from struggling lower-class neighborhood to slum accelerated.

Other Camps

The tent camp is obvious, easily read. It is a visual marker of both crisis and aid. To put it cynically, it photographs well and makes an easy narrative. But the camp cannot stand alone; it relies on other forms of humanitarian space in the city, the spatial and architectural products of the international institutions that dominate politics and daily life in Port-au-Prince. The camp is only the most obvious marker of the humanitarian crisis, but as such it misdirects attention from larger but less recognizable systems that support its existence.

The courtyard of the Hotel Karibe, where the government of Haiti, Deutsche Bank of the Americas Foundation, and the Clinton Global Initiative hosted the Building Back Better Communities Conference, a summit of design and construction firms and urban planners that focused on plans for rebuilding housing in Port-au-Prince.

In addition to the tarp-wrapped structures for those displaced by the earthquake, Port-au-Prince was host to another kind of camp in the wake of the earthquake. The most luxurious hotels of Port-au-Prince were transformed into de facto camps for another set of temporary inhabitants: the postdisaster influx of the international community. Karibe Hotel, Kinam Hotel, The Oloffson, each housed the foreign correspondents, politicians, aid workers, contractors, and consultants recently arrived to the city to deploy their expertise on those other, more publicized, camps.

These were the camps where we resided during our research visits to Haiti. We ate hotel meals with aid workers, held afternoon meetings on hotel patios, and attended the Building Back Better Communities Conference in a hotel full of international consultants, politicians, and journalists. In these hotel camps we overheard and engaged in conversations about the tent camps, their security challenges and public health issues, kidnappings, the threat of cholera, the seemingly impossible task of removing of the rubble. The financial costs and bureaucratic mechanisms of relief efforts in IDP tent communities were debated, and in some cases decided, from this set of hotel camps, which were sudden points of convergence for a host of international government and NGO workers. These hotel camps, in which we were uneasily implicated, acted as concentrators of power.

MINUSTAH, the Brazilian-led UN military force that arrived in Port-au-Prince in 2004 following the ouster of President Jean-Bertrand Aristide, bought out entire hotels to accommodate its troops. The peacekeepers also filled many of the city's upscale private residences, which saw a four-fold increase in rental prices in the months following the earthquake. The owners of these buildings were able to earn more by turning their spaces into a temporary barracks, a camp, than by staying open for standard business. At the marine port Terminal Varreux, two cruise ships full of UN staff and relief workers were docked in viewing distance of the teeming tent cities. These cruise ships, too, are camps. Though the forms are varied and have substantial and important differences, each of these camps is paid for and made possible by humanitarian aid, from the donation of tarps for shelter to the renting of a cruise ship or building to the cost of hotel accommodations for consultants.

In many cases, the ability of a form to disguise itself exists in direct correlation to its effectiveness in the city. The complexes of logistical hubs, industrial parks, and military command centers are also part of the architecture of humanitarianism, and architectural devices—towers, walls, guard posts, and gates—divide these spaces from the rest of the city. For each shelter built for an earthquake victim in Port-au-Prince, there exists a host of corresponding built urban forms that are inextricably linked and yet not readily apparent. For every television-ready refugee and aid worker, there are corresponding businessmen, consultants, politicians, gangsters, and soldiers who are equally influential agents of humanitarian urbanism and who are also architects of forms of aid.

TERRITORIES

Port-au-Prince, Haiti

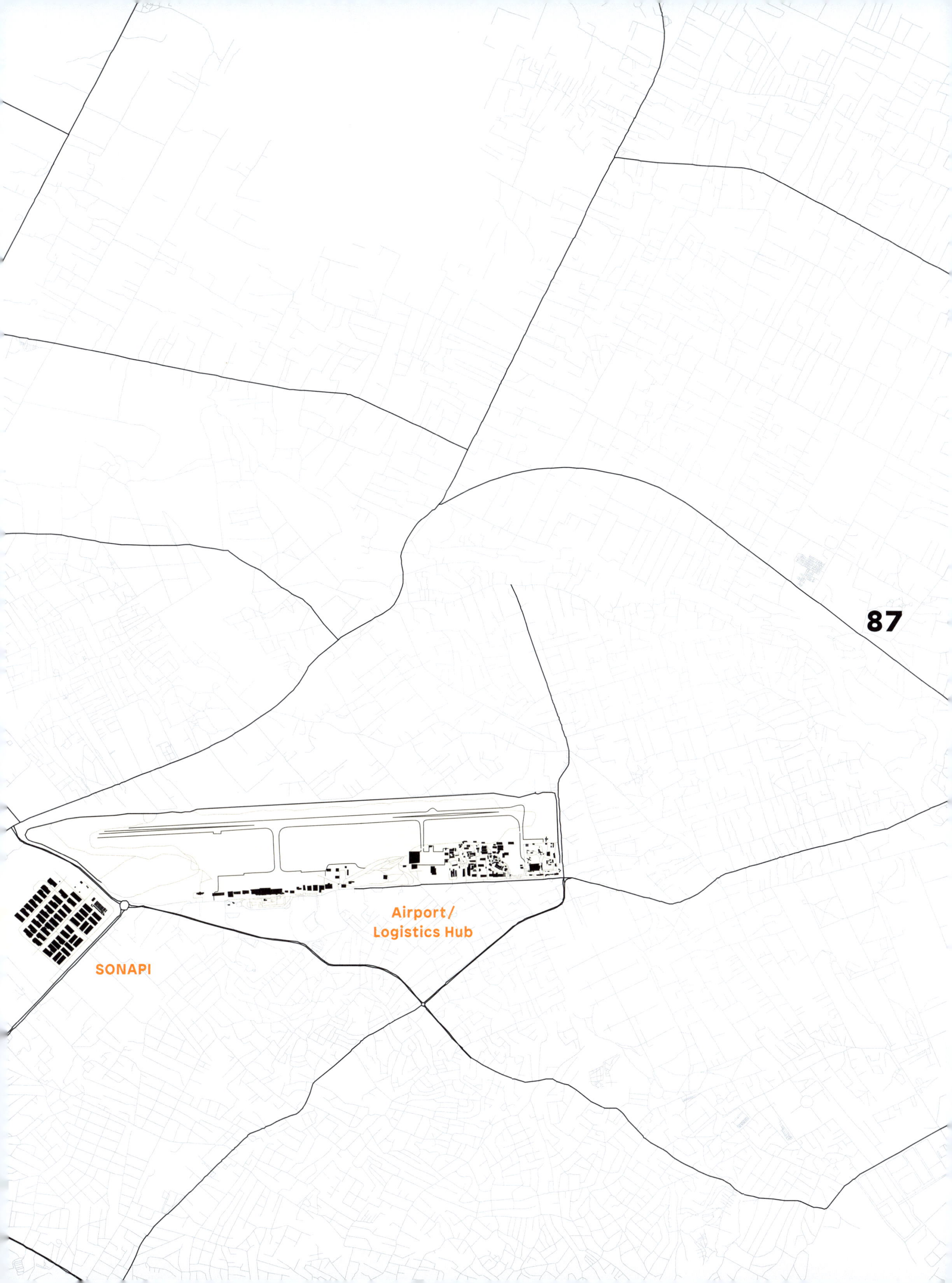
87
Airport/
Logistics Hub
SONAPI

Cité Soleil

Cité Soleil is Haiti's most well-known slum, and is one of the largest in the Americas, with an estimated 200,000 to 400,000 residents. The first neighborhoods of the area that became Cité Soleil were developed as a planned community of worker housing during François Duvalier's administration. After the ouster of President Aristide in 2004, Cité Soleil was the site of violent clashes between local groups (sometimes considered gangs) and the UN's MINUSTAH peacekeeping force. After the earthquake, it took at least two weeks for relief supplies to be delivered to Cité Soleil.

❶ Place Fierté, or Pride Park

The park was created during the Aristide administration, and required the clearing of dozens of houses in Cité Soleil. After the earthquake in 2010, the park quickly became an IDP camp, and remained so until 2012. In August 2012 MINUSTAH along with the Community Violence Reduction and Civil Affairs Sections announced the start of a $190,000 project to rebuild the park and create a community center. The tent camp was moved to the northwest of Cité Soleil.

2001.07.31

2003.10.08

2004.02.11

2010.01.24

2010.11.08

2012.03.26

❷ SHODECOSA

The SHODECOSA industrial park is owned by the Mevs family, a Haitian business dynasty that also owns Terminal Varreux. SHODECOSA provides warehouse services to the World Food Programme and other relief agencies that receive supplies from the port.

2003.10.08

2010.01.12

2012.03.26

2016.02.20

❸ Terminal Varreux

Owned by the Mevs family, Terminal Varreux is the main shipping and tanker port for Port-au-Prince.

2001.07.31

2010.01.12

2016.02.20

❹ BRABATT (Brazilian MINUSTAH compound)

The BRABATT (Brazilian Battalion) compound is the headquarters of MINUSTAH's operations in Cité Soleil.

2001.07.31

2003.12.19

2009.07.26

2010.08.17

2012.03.26

2016.02.20

❺ Cité Simone

The neighborhood of Cité Simone is the planned community from which Cité Soleil expanded, founded during François Duvalier's administration and named after the president's wife.

2001.07.31

2004.03.25

2006.01.29

2010.03.08

2016.02.20

❻ Relocated IDP community

After the clearing of the Place Fierté IDP camp in 2012, after two years of operation, the residents were relocated to this site on the marshy land that serves as Cité Soleil's sewer trench.

2003.10.08

2010.03.08

2012.03.26

2016.02.20

❼ Blue House

Formerly the residence and headquarters of prominent gang leader, Blue House was later a base of MINUSTAH's operations, as well as the site of a clean water distribution program.

2001.07.31

2009.07.26

2010.11.08

2016.02.20

SONAPI

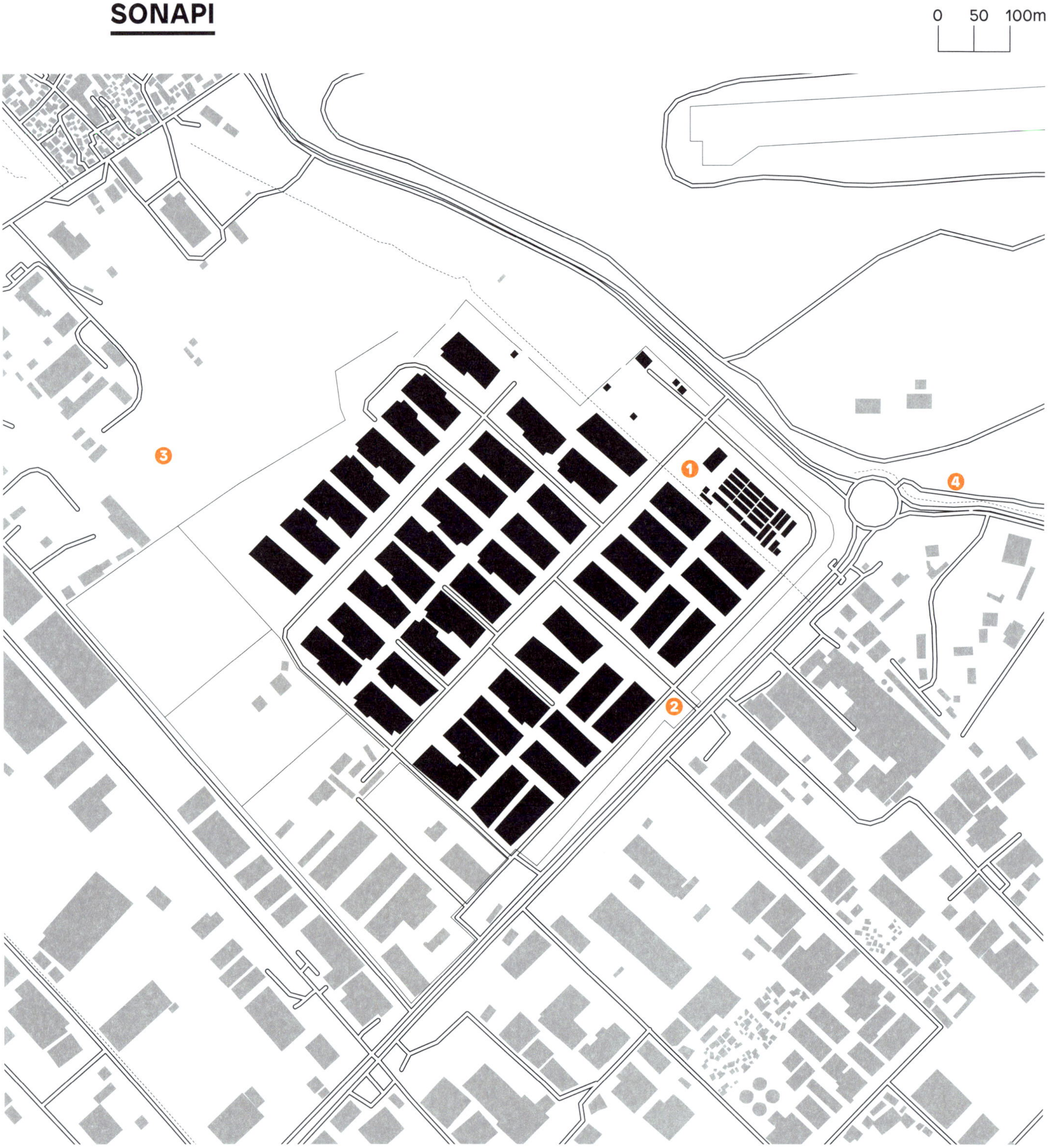

SONAPI is an export processing zone (EPZ) in Port-au-Prince. Companies in SONAPI pay no duties or direct taxes on their business activity. SONAPI has been the site of violent protests over working conditions, and is today guarded by MINUSTAH peacekeepers.

1 Haiti Apparel Center

The Haiti Apparel Center, a garment manufacturing training facility in SONAPI, was established with support and funding from USAID and several international NGOs, including the Clinton Global Initiative and CHF.

2009.07.26

2010.11.08

2012.09.15

2016.02.20

2 UN guard tower and SONAPI wall

Security at the SONAPI EPZ is provided by MINUSTAH peacekeepers.

2005.11.05

2010.11.08

2016.02.20

3 IDP camp

After the earthquake, a small tent camp was constructed in the yard behind SONAPI.

2004.11.15

2010.02.22

2012.03.26

2016.02.20

4 IDP camp and aid distribution point

An IDP camp filled the median of the road leading to the airport.

2009.07.26

2010.02.22

2010.08.17

2012.03.26

2016.02.20

Airport / Logistics Hub

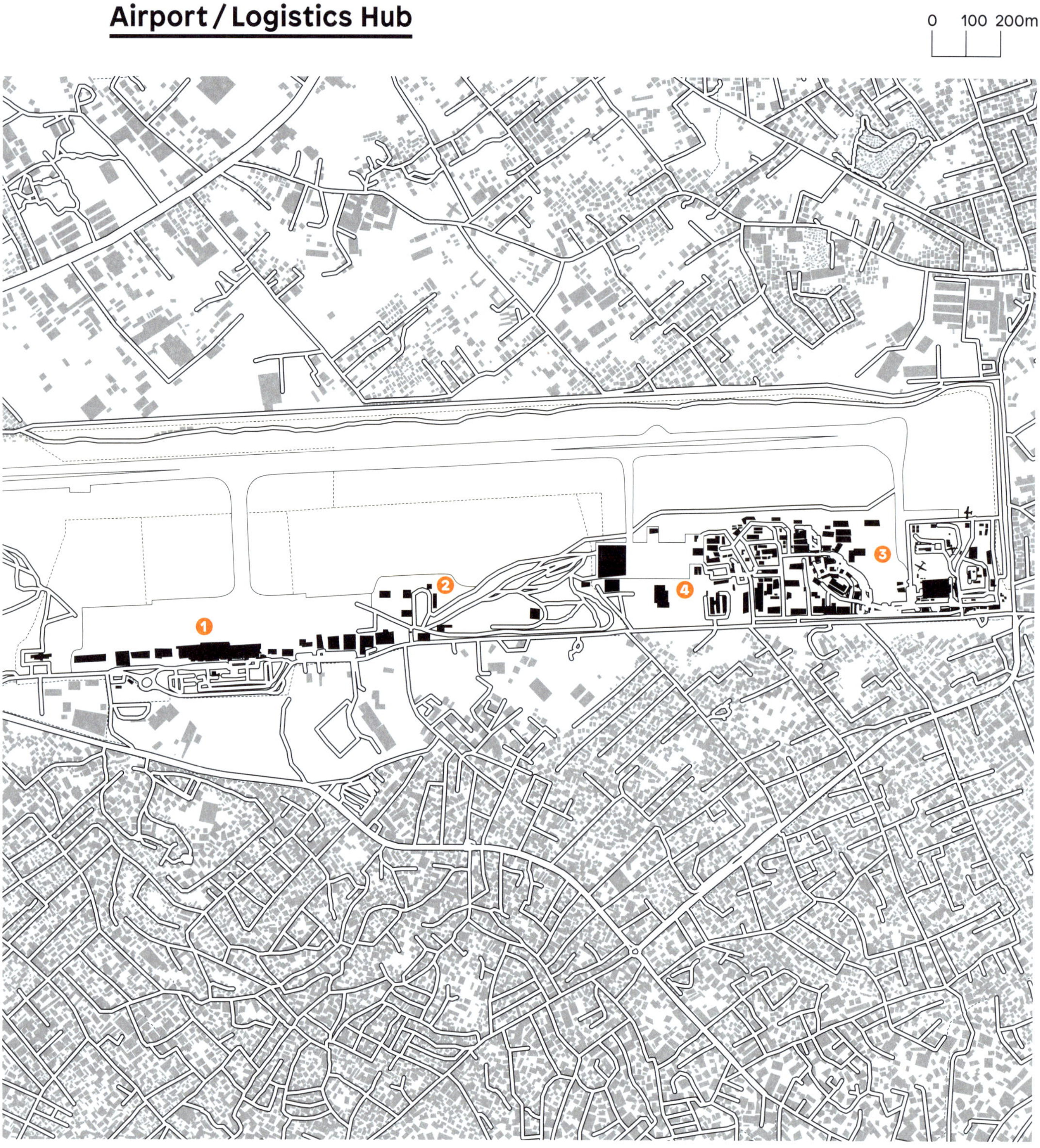

The Toussaint Louverture International Airport is an important channel through which relief operations are coordinated in Haiti, both before and after the 2010 earthquake.

Toussaint Louverture International Airport

Port-au-Prince's airport was developed with funding from the US during the Duvalier administration, and was initially named François Duvalier International Airport. The airport was heavily damaged during the earthquake, and its operations were temporarily turned over to the US military to coordinate the increased cargo traffic.

2003.10.08

2010.02.22

2016.02.20

Humanitarian Cargo Village

After the earthquake, a special area of the airport was dedicated to receiving and sorting shipments of relief supplies, with temporary logistical facilities established for many international NGOs.

2010.01.15

2010.01.26

2010.11.07

2016.02.20

UN Logistics Center

Since the start of the UN's MINUSTAH peacekeeping mission in 2004, part of the airport has been allocated for the UN's exclusive use.

2002.07.20

2005.09.30

2008.03.03

2010.03.08

2016.02.20

Mission Aviation Fellowship

The Mission Aviation Fellowship is a faith-based relief NGO that flies throughout Haiti supporting the efforts of Christian aid organizations, in operation since 1986.

2003.12.13

2008.03.03

2010.03.08

2016.02.20

Port Terminals

The port terminals are the channel through which much of the relief supplies that Haiti received after the earthquake entered the city.

1 Port International de Port-Au-Prince / Haiti Terminal S.A.

The international port suffered massive damage during the 2010 earthquake, but by 2015 was rebuilt and expanded on land reclaimed using rubble from the city's destroyed buildings.

2003.10.08

2010.11.08

2016.02.20

2 Iron Market

The Iron Market, a public market in the center of the city, was completely destroyed in the earthquake, but was rebuilt with charitable funding from Digicel, an Irish mobile telecom company that dominates the market in Haiti.

2002.09.17

2009.08.25

2010.11.08

2016.02.20

3 Centre Sportif IDP camp

After the earthquake, the Centre Sportif was filled with a sprawling tent camp, among the largest in Port-au-Prince and sheltering around 50,000 people.

2005.11.05

2010.01.16

2010.08.17

2013.04.15

2016.02.20

4 MSF Camp Mobile Clinic

Médecins sans Frontières operates a mobile clinic based in the camp.

2010.01.24

2010.11.08

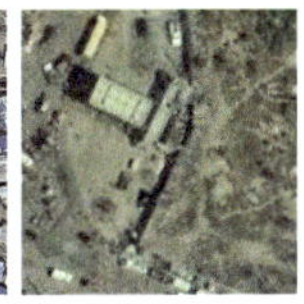
2016.02.20

5 Relocated IDP community

Following the clearing of many IDP camps in 2012, a cluster of transitional shelters was established on this site on the outskirts of the La Saline slum.

2009.07.26

2010.11.08

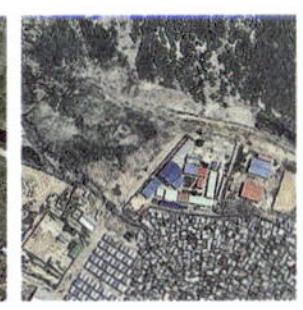
2013.09.10

2016.02.20

Zoranje

Zoranje is a new town north of Port-au-Prince, the site of several social housing projects since the 1990s. Most recently, it was the site of an exemplar community funded by a partnership between the Haitian government, Deutsche Bank of the Americas Foundation, and the Clinton Global Initiative.

1 Village du Renaissance

This social housing project was designed by Haitian architect, urban planner, and politician Leslie Voltaire during the Aristide administration. It was largely abandoned by the time the earthquake struck.

2004.02.11

2010.10.30

2016.02.20

2 Préval-era social housing

A second social housing block was constructed on the site toward the end of Arlstlde's presidency and continued during the presidency of René Préval.

2004.02.11

2010.11.08

2016.02.20

3 BBBC Expo Site

After the earthquake, the Haitian government partnered with the Deutsche Bank of the Americas Foundation and the Clinton Global Initiative to run an expo of prefabricated housing units. The project failed and the units were abandoned.

2010.01.08

2012.01.15

2016.02.20

4 Fonds d'assistance Economique et Sociale Site

The site was intended to be redeveloped in parallel with the BBBC Expo site as an exemplar community showcasing possibilities for Haiti's reconstruction, but due to budgetary and logistical limitations, the houses were never completed or even connected to utilities, and today remain unoccupied.

2010.11.08

2012.01.15

2016.02.20

5 Cuban-built social housing

During Aristide's presidency, housing was built with funding from the Cuban government.

2008.03.03

2009.07.26

2010.01.12

2016.02.20

3.
The West Bank and the Humanitarian-Security Complex

98

The year 1949 marked a double movement: the establishment of the provisional territorial limits of the state of Israel and the formation of the first UN agency to develop a working definition of *refugee*.[1] The drawing of the Green Line as part of the 1949 Armistice Agreements following the 1948 Arab-Israeli conflict and the founding of the United Nations Relief and Works Agency for Palestine Refugees in the Near East (UNRWA) were simultaneous processes, the creation of the state's territory coinciding with the designation of the refugee as a humanitarian subject.[2] The two figures, citizen and refugee, arose in an interdependent relationship. Corresponding to the two figures are two distinct but interrelated urban forms, the Israeli settlement and the Palestinian refugee camp.

1 The United Nations Relief and Works Agency for Palestine Refugees (UNRWA) predates the founding of the UN High Commissioner for Refugees (UNHCR) in 1950, as well as the United Nations Convention Relating to the Status of Refugees of 1951.

2 The definition used by UNRWA differs from the UNHCR definition, in that it allows for children of displaced persons to be considered refugees themselves. This definition has been criticized as perpetuating the conflict.

An IDF checkpoint in Hebron. The gate blocks Palestinian access to Shuhada Street, a Palestinian commercial area that has been closed since the 1990s. The building overlooking the checkpoint is Beit Romano, an Israeli settlement with a yeshiva and military outpost in Hebron.

While differing in urban morphology, arrangement of domestic units, and provision of infrastructure, the settlement and the refugee camp are alike in their efforts to recast the identities of their residents in direct relationship to the land without the intermediary of the nation-state. The settlements and refugee camps separate their populations from the territoriality of the state, and both settlement and camp persist in the same murky world of shifting boundaries and indefinite duration. The two emerge in relation to each other as twin forms in a spatiopolitical complex comprised of camp and settlement, and with them networks of relief and support to sustain a condition of near permanent almost-crisis.

The refugee camp and the settlement are conjoined and inseparable, two mutually reinforcing spatial types that are defined by the militarization of their domestic routines and distinguished by the extraterritorial status of their spaces and their corresponding populations. Both the settlement and the refugee camp practice a kind of temporal and legal suspension in which they claim to be temporary even as all of the evidence suggests otherwise. While ostensibly impermanent in their built form, they continue to endure and expand, build and rebuild. They are extraterritorial spaces insofar as their residents are either stateless or living outside the nominal boundaries of the state in a contested area whose status is continually debated in the UN, as many of its member states continue to financially support either side, and sometimes both sides. The camps and the settlements are subsidized and funded by humanitarian organizations, NGOs, private foundations, and individual donors, as well as by national governments and international institutions. Both communities are linked to their neighbors by a history of displacement and find justification in the words and material support of foreign nations. Both the settlement and the refugee camp are forms of aid.

Dheisheh, the Camps

The Palestinian camps are nexuses of international humanitarian operations. While administered and policed by the Palestinian National Authority, many of their social services are sustained by UNRWA's continuing assistance in providing schools, health programs, water infrastructure, and food relief. During the Second Intifada, beginning September 2000, the UN Office for the Coordination of Humanitarian Affairs (UN-OCHA), the United Arab Emirates Red Crescent Society, and the United States Agency for International Development (USAID) also coordinated emergency humanitarian operations. UNRWA is the only top-level UN organization that is region-specific; while the UNHCR focuses its efforts on temporarily displaced communities around the world, UNRWA is unique among UN organizations in that it directs its attention and resources exclusively to sustaining the displaced Palestinian community, the first refugees to be defined as such by the UN shortly after its own creation. The differences in the two organizations, the intensity of their operations and expenditures, is stark. As of 2015, UNRWA's area staff of 30,718,[3] many of them Palestinians, is almost three times that of the UNHCR,[4] the UN agency responsible for all other refugees worldwide. As measured by staffing, the intensity of international aid through the United Nations to the Palestinian refugee community is unparalleled. UNRWA's 2015 total expenses ($1,333,800,000)[5] were almost half the total of UNHCR's worldwide expenditures ($3,288,140,248) the same year, and exceeded UNHCR's expenditures in any single region of operation (Africa, the Americas, Asia and the Pacific, Europe, or the Middle East and North Africa).[6]

3 United Nations Relief and Works Agency, "UNRWA in Figures, as of Jan 1 2015," goo.gl/yxK45T.

4 United Nations High Commissioner for Refugees, "Figures at a Glance," goo.gl/bmUq3O.

5 United Nations Relief and Works Agency, "Annual Operational Report 2015," goo.gltzQ3Qf.

6 United Nations High Commissioner for Refugees, "Financials," goo.gl/Z2hEuW.

The sustained support and development aid from international donors, channeled through UNRWA to the material and infrastructural support of Palestinian refugee camps and their residents for more than sixty years, has constructed and maintained the spatial form of the camp as well as the refugee as a figure. Unlike other humanitarian crises and their resulting camps, whose temporary condition has been extended due to prolonged military or environmental crises, in the West Bank the camp and the refugee have been continually redefined by humanitarian aid organizations, and the lifespan of the category of the refugee has been extended through bureaucratic measures. Diverging from UNHCR's definition of a refugee as "someone who has been forced to flee his or her country because of persecution, war, or violence,"[7] UNRWA also considers the patrilineal descendants of the refugees of the wars in 1948 and 1967 as refugees. This is the camp on hyperdrive, extending both its temporal boundaries and the scope of its activity.

7 United Nations High Commissioner for Refugees, "What is a Refugee?," goo.gl/byhHH6.

Alessandro Petti, cofounder with Sandi Hilal of Campus in Camps in the Dheisheh refugee camp, writes that in the West Bank the camps have been transformed into "permanent expressions of ideology and power," and that "whether they serve temporarily or become more permanent is ultimately not decided by the humanitarian bodies tasked with managing and controlling them, but rather by political conflicts."[8] We agree with Petti's premise that the extension of a camp's temporary life cycle is, of course, connected to its political situation, but we would suggest that the relief organizations who manage and control these spaces, who construct and reconstruct the conditions of life within the Occupied Palestinian Territories, are not separable from the political conflict, and are implicated in the spatial forms that result. We see the camp as not only a conceptual category, but a physical site with a definite urban form and social relations sustained through humanitarian aid, which is never, finally, an entirely apolitical form of life support. If, as Giorgio Agamben wrote, the camp is the site where political subjects are reduced to bare life, then those organizations tasked with sustaining and administering that life must be responsible for the outcomes of their efforts, both on the city, the individual, and society.

8 Alessandro Petti, "Architecture of Exile," *Campus in Camps*, January 2015, goo.gl/SQFGjD.

There are many contemporary and historical cases where the residents of a refugee camp are eager to leave the camp and establish a permanent home in a new country, removed both from the dire conditions of the camp and from the violence exercised over a territory and population that pushed them into the camp in the first place. We are now seeing this desire play out in the massive migrations of Syrian refugees moving across Europe, seeking both physical and legal asylum in new nations. These refugees seek permanent relocation within the legal and geographical bounds of the state that receives them, allowing them to escape both the devastation of their home country and the limbo of the camps that have flourished at train stations, border crossings, and beach towns across Europe. Their struggle is to leave the camp for a new life in the city. In the West Bank, the struggle of many refugees is different: to refuse the city and insist on the camp.

There are occasions and conditions when a camp is preferable to a city, when a temporary shelter is better than a new house, and cultivating a

A view from the top of the hill on which Dheisheh is built

kind of dwelling in displacement can be better than normalizing an oppressive routine. For the residents of Dheisheh, the oldest refugee camp in the West Bank, insistence on the temporary nature of the camp and the refugees' right to return to their original forty-five villages is a means of resistance and of preserving self-identity and social connections. Their position has strong international support, and the Palestinian right to return has been recognized by UN General Assembly Resolutions 194 in 1948 and 3236 in 1974.[9] Their insistence on the prolongation of their refugee status has had architectural consequences that are registered in the form of the Palestinian camps.

9 In 1948 the United Nations General Assembly adopted Resolution 194 (III), resolving that "refugees wishing to return to their homes and live at peace with their neighbours should be permitted to do so at the earliest practicable date, and that compensation should be paid for the property of those choosing not to return and for loss of or damage to property which, under principles of international law or equity, should be made good by the Governments or authorities responsible." UN, Resolution 194, December 11, 1948, goo.gl/AOTso2.

Dheisheh was the first Palestinian refugee camp established following the 1948 Arab-Israeli War, built on land leased from the Jordanian government. Initially, the shelters consisted only of canvas tents, and the perimeter of the camp was enclosed by a fence and entered through a single metal turnstile gate. In the late 1950s the UN began to upgrade the camp to more permanent shelters. Despite spending more than ten years in tents after the 1948 war, the residents of Dheisheh initially resisted the UN's efforts to provide seemingly more humane housing in the form of concrete walled units, 10 square meters in area, with rough floors and metal roofs. Similarly, in the Balata camp in northern West Bank, where the UN began offering similar housing to refugees beginning in 1950, many refugees refused the offer of more permanent, solid, and weatherproof structures, which were seen to symbolize an acceptance of their permanent relocation. Their rejection of architecture and infrastructure was a means of protest—a refusal to normalize the conditions of their dislocation, to insist that their status as refugees be acknowledged as an effect of an ongoing political conflict rather than a humanitarian crisis. Nevertheless, the concrete boxes were built by UNRWA as a form of humanitarian aid and placed directly on the plots of land originally allocated to the tents. Dheisheh was cramped even then and remains overcrowded with residents today, many of whom continue to consider themselves as the displaced residents of villages destroyed or occupied by Israel since 1948. Because UNRWA's legal definition of the Palestinians' refugee status allows it to be transferred through generations, humanitarian aid perpetuates an inheritance of spatial dislocation.

Like many refugee camps in the West Bank, Dheisheh became weightier, more solid, and more permanent as the camp grew: first tents, then the UN's small concrete shelters, followed by single-story and then multistory buildings built by the refugees. According to UNRWA's records, 845 shelters were built at the camp's establishment, and 1,550 buildings were counted by UNRWA in 2005, resulting in a total density as measured by floor space index of 0.95. The vertical expansion of the camp has stretched the footprint of the original single-story shelters upward to varying heights: only 10 percent of structures remain a single story, while 60 percent reach three stories and 20 percent reach

One of the original 10 m^2 concrete blocks (left) that were constructed in the 1950s by UNRWA. This unit was subsequently expanded by its occupants.

four or more stories. Commercial activity, mostly concentrated at the outer edge of the camp close to Hebron Road, is largely owned and operated by outsiders: only 30 percent of the 200 commercial businesses counted in 2007 within Dheisheh were owned by camp residents.[10] The construction materials prevalent in Dheisheh are heavy and solid: more than 87 percent are built from cement brick and more than 10 percent are built from stone.[11] More than politics, UN resolutions, or the passage of time, architecture has made the refugee camps in the West Bank appear as a persistent reality. The camps exist now as a built paradox, heavily subsidized and highly visible spaces whose poor physical condition serves as a visual insistence on the Palestinian right of return. However, in Dheisheh, the pressures and discomforts of sixty years' residence in a refugee camp have caused some residents to direct their energies toward forming a new town, both an extension and an antithesis to the camp, sited across the road from Dheisheh.

10 United Nations Relief and Works Agency, "Dheisheh Refugee Camp Profile," October 2008, 5, goo.gl/DltSDU.

11 Ibid., 3.

Crossing Hebron Road, the town of Doha spreads across the hillside with large and expansive houses, the generous spacing between buildings a stark contrast to the cramped narrow streets in Dheisheh.[12] Doha and Dheisheh face one another across a small valley where Hebron road runs along the bottom, and thus many residences at the upper elevations have clear views to the other community, reinforcing the sense of a conjoined and oppositional relationship between two cities. Doha was also created through aid, albeit under different circumstances than Dheisheh. The town was formerly a part of the territory of the Palestinian municipality of Beit Jala until 1977, when the mayor of Beit Jala visited Qatar and secured a large donation from the royal family, subsequently renaming a portion of its municipality for the Qatar capital, Doha, as a gesture of gratitude. Doha became an independent municipality in 1996, after the 1993 Oslo accords released Beit Jala from Israeli governance.

12 Doha, alternately spelled Al-Dawha and Ad-Doha, is north of Dheisheh across Hebron Road, and is named after a street in the Beit Jala neighborhood that was financed with aid from Doha, Qatar.

After an afternoon walking through Dheisheh with a local guide, he invited us to his family home across the road in Doha, to get a better sense of life in the town. As we wound our way up the hill into Doha, we observed a marked change in material quality and architectural detail, from the wider spacing between buildings to the inclusion of garages for vehicles. Doha is a refugee city, a logical consequence of the quasipermanence of the Palestinians' refugee status that simultaneously allows a measure of normalcy in living standards while maintaining Dheisheh's status as a camp, both symbolically and materially: a space that resists being resettled and asserts a continuing right of return, a right to consider the camp temporary in spite of all evidence to the contrary.

Dheisheh and Doha are part of the larger temporal and spatial suspension of the West Bank's territorial organization, stemming in part from the indeterminacy of the Green Line, the demarcation set out by the 1949 Armistice Agreements as the de facto boundary of the state of Israel. After the 1967 Six-Day War the status of the Green Line, which was never ratified as a permanent territorial border, became uncertain. The line became the subject of a political debate about the future of any border between Israel and the West Bank, leading to the current situation in which elaborate technologies operating at a territorial scale maintain the separation between Palestinian areas and Israeli settlements in the West Bank.

The Green Line and the Settlements

If, in architecture, the drawing of a line is a moment of decision, the fixing of a conceptual boundary in a concrete and ideally permanent form, the Green Line has a paradoxical effect, producing instead an enduring suspension of the boundaries of the state.[13]

13 The Green Line is a cease-fire agreement, not an international or permanent boundary. It preserves the territorial claims of all the parties (Egypt, Lebanon, Jordan, and Syria) without establishing borders between them.

The provisional status of the Green Line allows the State of Israel to continually modify the operational extents of its territory, drawing the line between areas administered by the state and those controlled by the Israeli military and the Palestinian National Authority. The effect of the Green Line is to establish the permanence of the state within its limits, while subjecting the areas outside to a persistently temporary status. The line inaugurates a host of spatial practices that enable both Israeli settlers and Palestinian refugees to maneuver through and within this indefinitely temporary condition. The movements and daily routines in both the Israeli settlements and the Palestinian towns and refugee camps are conditioned by this intangible, invisible delineation.

Not all humanitarian shelters are as readily recognizable as the residences in a refugee camp. The suburban pastoralism of the settlement of El'azar makes it seem like an idyllic community, albeit one with armed guards at the entrances, located on an Israeli-only access road. Just as the refusal of a permanent home is crucial in Dheisheh, it is equally important to construct the illusion of hypernormative stability within the settlements. The settlements require an architecture that looks at home, an arguably theatrical performance of domesticity which incorporates territory through an aggressive banality, the presumption of belonging visually communicated by repetitive rows of single-family homes, offering a sharp contrast to the self-built houses of Palestinians unable to procure building permits in the West Bank.

In the settlements of Etzion Bloc, suburban lanes lined with well-kept houses do not betray their extraterritorial condition or the support of international charities. There are no foundation logos plastered on their facades, like the temporary shelters in most refugee communities. These are hypernormative structures whose architectural forms echo familiar suburban layouts, lining culs-de-sac and providing outward-looking views across the desert valley.

It takes time for settlements to develop this level of architectural permanence, and most have begun as far less comfortable and more explicitly militarized operations. The architect Sharon Rotbard has explored the origins of Israeli settlements in the Homa Umigdal (wall and tower) project begun in 1936 by members of Kibbutz Tel Amal as "a system of settlement seemingly defensive but essentially of offensive form."[14] This effort to initiate new settlements began with the construction of a wall (militarized defense), followed by a tower (surveillance), and lastly, residences (domesticated occupation). The construction sequence of Homa Umigdal first prioritizes security and defensibility, followed by the erection of the tower as a vantage point, an instrumentalization of the gaze across a landscape understood as potentially hostile territory, and finally domestication through the construction of homes.

14 Sharon Rotbard, "Wall and Tower (Homa Umigdal)" in *A Civilian Occupation*, ed. Rafi Segal and Eyal Weizman (New York: Verso Press, 2003), 42.

Traveling throughout the West Bank in 2013, we visited settlements in various stages of construction and expansion, undergoing the process of transformation from paramilitary outpost to permanent settlement that has been more or less continuous since the mid-1930s. These spaces owe their formal logic to the Homa Umigdal project, beginning as lone trailers flying the Israeli flag on a hilltop, then aggregating to form a circle of trailers enclosed by a barbed wire fence and security lights, before solidifying to the weighty suburban tract homes of the most established settlements. There is a material shedding process in this series of state changes, accompanied by the collection and manipulation of heavier materials, a move from prefabricated elements to those requiring site construction and more durable infrastructure. Where there was once a prefabricated trailer, a foundation is poured, and eventually a home is constructed. What was once an outpost or an encampment is now a residential community. Yet the forms of military occupation remain, the walls and gates and towers, and there is as much ambiguity in the transition from camp to home as from militant to civilian.

At the scale of the Israeli-Palestinian conflict, the construction of settlements—vantage points plotted like so many stars across the landscape of the West Bank—forms a disruptive network, a strategic constellation intended to thwart the possibility of a contiguous Palestinian State. Occupation of these settlements is both a violation of international law and a fact of everyday life which is unlikely to change very much in the foreseeable future, particularly with the Israeli government under Benjamin Netanyahu authorizing the construction of new settlements in early 2017. The settlements are like so many outposts, inhabited by civilians whose daily lives are mobilized as part of a violent territorial conflict. The schizophrenic military-civilian life of the settlements is materialized in their urban form, wherein the relationship of the residents to the neighboring

Palestinian areas is articulated through a series of walls, towers, and gates played out at a territorial scale, a contemporary organization that betrays a debt to the Homa Umigdal, but has escaped the limited geographical dimensions of the encampment and has merged with the landscape of the West Bank.

Outside of the internationally recognized territory of the Israeli state and yet continually mobilized in service of its leaders' political ends, the settlements are considered to be "no less valuable than a military unit"[15] by high-ranking officials. By extension, the settlements' residents could be considered a strange and subtle army. The settlements exist as a vital component of a militarized occupation, and yet they include all the markers of ordinary life: playgrounds, temples, hospitals, video stores. Under a perpetual assumption of potential siege, their extraterritorial security is maintained not only by Israeli Defense Forces (IDF) soldiers, but also by families, teenagers, tourists, and schoolchildren.

15 Yigal Allon, *Curtain of Sand* (Tel Aviv: Hakibbutz Hameuchad, 1998 [1959]), 244.

An IDF guard tower overlooking Highway 60 between Bethlehem and Hebron

16 Malkah Fleisher, "New Immigrants to Gush Etzion Receive Extra Help," *Arutz Sheva*, May 25, 2009, goo.gl/gHVE98.

17 Information about the Israel Forever Foundation's Virtual Citizen of Israel program is available at goo.gl/w4d1dH.

The illusion of normality in the settlements is underwritten by streams of international aid, both official development assistance (ODA) from foreign governments and money from charitable foundations, many of which are based in the US. Settlers are encouraged to populate the West Bank not only through religious and nationalist rhetoric, but by the provision of financial and social support both within Israel and abroad. As of 2009, new immigrants to communities in the Gush Etzion area of the Judean region receive additional benefits and support as part of the Aliyah Kehilati "Community Aliyah" program, headed by the nonprofit Nefesh B'Nefesh in partnership with the Israeli Ministry of Immigrant Absorption.[16] Nefesh B'Nefesh offers significant financial and logistical support to the *olim* (immigrants making aliyah to Israel), facilitating settlement growth throughout the West Bank through international migration and heavily subsidized rents in settlements beyond the Green Line. For those who are unable to make aliyah and physically relocate to the settlements but nonetheless wish to express support, there are other options. In this contested territory, the Israel Forever Foundation offers a virtual citizenship program that includes a certificate of "virtual residence" in Israel, a digital aliyah.[17]

The settlements in the Etzion Bloc are directly supported by allied foundations abroad. Founded in 1993, the Gush Etzion Foundation is an independent nonprofit that "approaches donors in Israel and overseas, keeping them updated about ongoing needs and new initiatives in the area."[18] The foundation is classified as an international development and relief service by the National Taxonomy of Exempt Entities (NTEE) system used by the IRS to classify nonprofit organizations, and is tax-exempt in the United States.[19] Its projects bear similarities to the work of UNRWA in the refugee camps: provision of direct financial aid to families, provision of food packages, the funding and furnishing of schools and educational programs, and the creation of playgrounds and parks. Additionally, the foundation maintains rescue teams and emergency medical services, purchases security equipment, and funded construction of the Pina Chama (translated into English by the foundation as "Cozy Corner") at the Gush Etzion Junction, a rest stop for IDF soldiers that serves food and drink and is staffed by volunteers from the local settlements. That this blend of ideologically driven "communal hospitality" (their term) for military support services, funded by international donations, occurs within an unassuming restaurant at a highway intersection illustrates the shape-shifting quality of humanitarian spaces created by international aid.

18 "Our Vision: Preserving the History and Heritage, Building the Future, Strengthening the Community," *The Gush Etzion Foundation*, goo.gl/IBQeHZ.

19 ProPublica Nonprofit Explorer, "Gush Etzion Foundation," *ProPublica*, goo.gl/82Xc72.

A view from Nokdim toward the group of caravans and houses known as Tekoa D, an illegal outpost

Like the Palestinian refugee camps, Israeli settlements are dependent on international support, both private and governmental. Despite being a relatively wealthy country, Israel was the single largest recipient of international ODA between the years 1970 and 1995, receiving about $400 per capita annually during a period throughout which it consistently pursued a policy of settlement building in the West Bank.[20] This aid was granted in 1967 after Israel's claims to territory had expanded beyond the boundaries recognized by international law, violating the Geneva Convention by transferring population to a zone of military occupation. The UN Security Council has taken the view that such policy and practices "have no legal validity" and constitute a "flagrant violation" of the Convention.[21] Whatever one's opinion regarding the justification or lack thereof for Israel's expansion of its national boundaries, the reality of the simultaneous condemnation of settlement building by the UN Security Council and the steady influx of development aid remains an evident contradiction, one that has materialized in the architectural facts on the ground. Construction of settlements and infrastructure throughout the West Bank during this period was in effect partially funded by US development assistance to the Israeli government, a gesture tied to Israel's strategic position in relation to US interests in the Middle East. The current crisis in the West Bank has been made possible, constructed, and maintained by aid.

20 Alberto Alesina and David Dollar, "Who Gives to Foreign Aid and Why?," *Journal of Economic Growth* 5, no. 1 (2000); Journal of Economic Growth 5, no. 1, 40.

21 International Court of Justice (ICJ), case, Legal Consequences of the Construction of a Wall in the Occupied Palestinian Territory, "Summary of the Advisory Opinion of 9 July 2004," 10, goo.gl/rEhohh.

On the ground in the West Bank, streams of aid are transformed through construction into cities and roads, schools, and airstrips. Development of the settlements is encouraged by the Israeli government through various mechanisms, including reduced property taxes, grant subsidies for land acquisition, preferential loans given to settlers and industrial investors, and the construction of highways and infrastructure.[22] They are also sustained by charities in the United States that raise funds among the Jewish community and American evangelicals in support of schools and synagogues and also bulletproof vests and guard dogs for the settlements.[23] In many ways, what are considered flaws in the operational abilities of private nonprofits in other contexts become assets in the construction and maintenance of the Israeli settlements. Without being beholden to any comprehensive master plan or regional administration, these small charities are able to directly shape the facts on the ground and thus construct new physical and political landscapes in which to conduct their operations.

22 See "Land Expropriation and Settlements," *B'Tselem*, January 1, 2011, last updated November 23, 2015, goo.gl/tFTHTh.

23 Jim Rutenberg, Mike McIntire, and Ethan Bronner, "Tax-Exempt Funds Aid Settlements in West Bank," *New York Times*, July 5, 2010, goo.gl/jrXYaY. The use of tax-free donations made through private charities to fund settlements places the US Treasury at odds with the State Department, effectively providing government subsidy for settlements in contradiction of the position of the administration.

Our passage into and among the Israeli settlements was fluid and direct, if a little unnerving due the proportion of our fellow passengers who were heavily armed teenagers fulfilling their mandatory service in the IDF. Looking out of the windows of one of the buses connecting the Gush Etzion settlement bloc with service to Jerusalem, a series of Palestinian areas were visible through the dusty glass, passing by and fading out of sight. They were fleeting visions from our bus as we traveled Highway 60, visible and yet inaccessible, because this portion of Highway 60 is restricted to vehicles with yellow (Israeli) license plates, while the other roads, leading to the Palestinian areas, are sanctioned for use only by cars with green (Palestinian) plates.

Such road restrictions speed the movement between settlement areas of the West Bank as part of an infrastructural network that is doubled, whose twists and turns respond to the presence of the other without intersection.

A sign on a road leading into Area A (the designation for territory controlled by the Palestinian National Authority) forbids Israeli citizens to enter.

In the West Bank, parallel realities are navigable by separate infrastructures: one network for Palestinians and another network for Israelis, overlapping at points of spatial and economic necessity, and then peeling off again. These separate infrastructures create vastly different scalar relationships between the shared landscape and the segregated travelers; winding routes, detours, and construction quality make movement ponderously slow for many Palestinians while continual government-funded upgrades keep the highways to the settlements rapid and efficient, encouraging further growth. The roads, while they are fixed in physical space, have brought distant parts of the country closer through construction of two separate spatiotemporal architectures. These roads serve as lines to connect and thus incorporate West Bank territories into the Israeli state, at least functionally if not by law. For example, Route 398 creates a short circuit between Jerusalem and a string of Israeli settlements, including Nokdim. Route 398, a bypass road which is also known as Lieberman Road after Avigdor Lieberman, minister of construction and housing under Ariel Sharon and a resident of Nokdim, branches off Highway 60 close to Jerusalem as it heads toward the settlement, shortening a commute which previously took forty-five minutes winding through Palestinian communities into a ten-minute drive bypassing those areas and running directly to Jerusalem. Since Route 398 opened to traffic in 2008, the Israeli populations of the settlements served by this road have grown 90 percent, according to an analysis of data from the Israeli Central Bureau of Statistics analyzed by Peace Now.[24] Such a direct demographic response to the construction of infrastructure networks is evidence of the Israeli urban planning efforts tacitly enabling the deployment of civilian bodies in the occupation of disputed territory via settlements.

24 "The Impact of Bypass Roads on the Development of Settlements," *Peace Now*, October 7, 2015, goo.gl/ZeqJlt.

Taking the system of Israeli buses throughout the West Bank, we traveled with unexpected ease from the Egged Terminal in Jerusalem, with its noisy food courts and crowds awaiting their departures, to Atzei HaZayit Square in Nokdim, a silent cul-de-sac surrounded by empty streets. Passing through the guard post, the 166 bus line carried us smoothly through a gate manned by IDF soldiers and into the residential community, a small suburb with the atmosphere of a closed military zone.

The layout of Nokdim follows the principals of optical planning in the design of settlements, as described by Rafi Segal and Eyal Weizman. Segal and Weizman analyzed Israeli Ministry of Construction and Housing manuals from the 1980s and found them to be primarily concerned with the layout of housing in relationship to the views afforded by turning the building to align with the slope. They summarize their analysis, "Urban layout that follows topographical lines around the mountain summit is contingent with the principle of maximizing the view. [...] The inward-oriented gaze protects the soft cores of the settlements, and the outward-oriented one surveys the landscape around it."[25] With its sharp hills and deep valleys, the landscape of the West Bank provides ample opportunity for the capture of vision through design of the built environment. The topography orchestrates sectional relationships, which are reinforced by the placement and orientation of settlements, infrastructure, roads, and checkpoints. Architecture designed for this landscape exploits the topography of the hills and valleys, enlisting the natural environment as a territorial strategy.

25 Rafi Segal and Eyal Weizman, "The Mountain," in *A Civilian Occupation*, 85 (see note 14).

As in many settlements, the orientation of the houses in El'azar follows the contour lines of the hill on which the settlement is built, so that the houses have clear sight lines across the surrounding valley, combining visual control of a potentially hostile environment with scenic views.

A street in Nokdim, an Israeli settlement of about 2,000 people in the Etzion Bloc in the West Bank

What appear to be placid suburban communities are thus also defensive towers acting in the Israeli national security interest: each home is aligned perpendicular to the slope of the terrain to provide views of the surrounding territories. This urban strategy is an extension of the principles of linear perspectival drawing, a means of architectural representation that implicates the viewer in the image. The settlements, designed in anticipation of the viewing inhabitant, use the principles of perspective to place the settlers in the landscape and engage them with the surrounding territories. This mastery of landscape through the orchestration of vision is the defining urban characteristic of the settlement as a form of tower.

The typology of city-as-tower was formalized by inclusion in *Building and Development in the Mountain Regions*, a handbook produced by the Ministry of Construction and Housing in 1984 and discussed by Segal and Weizman,[26] which emphasized layouts that maximized outward vision, down to the organization of internal spaces and placement of windows.[27] In the West Bank, the settlement is both fortress and neighborhood, panopticon and suburban idyll. It is a place where you feel simultaneously at home and under siege, a domesticated military outpost. The front lines are a living boundary of the occupation that constitutes the territory, a biological mobilization of everyday life in the service of territorial expansion. Here, the daily commute is a patrol, the view from the living room is defensive surveillance, and children on a playground are an occupying force.

26 Segal and Weizman provide a brief explanation of the movement of settlements to the hills as driven by a militarized urban planning strategy, using the topography of the West Bank to secure high points for military advantage.

27 Michael Boneh, *Building and Development in the Mountain Regions* (Jerusalem: Ministry of Construction and Housing, 1984), Cited in Eyal Weizman, *Hollow Land* (London: Verso, 2007).

Contemporary hilltop settlements in the West Bank deploy the design logic of the early Zionist Homa Umigdal towers at a greatly enlarged scale, pursuing dual strategies of enclosure and surveillance to expand their territory without bounds. Defensive vision is fundamental to the strategy of the settlements, a tenet reiterated by government officials, military commanders, and urban planners alike. Israeli deployment of vision in the maintenance of perpetual conflict is necessarily a one-way mechanism; according to official military guidelines, any Palestinian caught looking at a settlement with binoculars or in a suspicious manner may be shot and killed.[28] In the West Bank, vision is a powerful and dangerous weapon.

28 Amos Harel, "Soldiers Can Shoot Gazans Spying on Netzarim," *Ha'aretz*, November 5, 2003, goo.gl/cB45QS.

Control of physical space through visual mechanisms occurs throughout the West Bank in various guises and at multiple scales. It is present in the organization of the refugee camps and settlements alike, instrumentalizing individuals' vision toward the maintenance of large-scale territorial relationships. In Hebron, the construction of numerous Israeli settlements within, above, and beside the Palestinian city has built a sort of Gordian knot of mutual surveillance and violence codified through built space.

Hebron

The old town of Hebron is characterized by a tangle of alleys, covered passageways, internal courtyards, arches, stone walls, and decorated apertures. Within this density of Palestinian residential and commercial areas are multiple Israeli settlements, exponentially increasing the spatial complexity of segregated districts and their technologies of separation: barriers, border zones, checkpoints, and watchtowers.

Some of the Israeli settlements in Hebron exist only at the upper level of a neighborhood, while the ground level is occupied by Palestinians, creating a vertical stratification and separation. In those areas, dense metal mesh like that used in animal fencing stretches over metal beams to divide the air above pedestrian passages, catching objects tossed by settlers onto the streets below. Watchtowers staffed by young IDF recruits are scattered across the rooftops, their surveillance work supplemented by video security cameras. Checkpoints separate the horizontal continuity of the roads and sidewalks, modulating the flow of goods and bodies, and numerous streets dead-end in thick concrete barriers, signaling the edge of a settlement or segregated road. Some of the barriers include thick steel doors in cast concrete frames, with tiny windows of bulletproof glass to allow for controlled movement and views to the other side.

An IDF guard post on a rooftop in an Israeli-controlled area of Hebron.

The barriers we encountered walking through the city were decorated by a range of murals, semiofficial interpretive signage, multilingual graffiti laced with epithets, and what appeared to be paintball splatters. Where the streets dead-ended into a concrete barrier, we frequently found dumping grounds and colonies of feral cats. In one location, the street leading up to the barrier was fenced off to create an enclosure for domesticated ducks and geese: the ground-level shops flanking the street had been converted to an abattoir. At another site, a swinging wooden bench had been built into the concrete barricade wall in what felt like a comically romantic appropriation of the technologies of segregation.

The Israeli settlement Beit Hadassah in Hebron is on the second floor of buildings whose ground level is a Palestinian market. Metal grills prevent settlers from dropping objects or trash on the market.

Hebron is the only Palestinian city in the West Bank that was not transferred to Palestinian control during the Oslo Accords, but was instead transferred under a separate agreement signed in 1997 between the Israeli government under the administration of Benjamin Netanyahu and the Palestinian Liberation Organization under the administration of Yasser Arafat. The agreement, referred to as the Hebron Protocol, designated approximately 80 percent of the land as H-1 areas under Palestinian control while the remaining 20 percent remained H-2 areas under Israeli control. These separate zones, H-1 and H-2, persist today and continue to shape the social life and built environment of Hebron. Within the security arrangements enumerated by the Hebron Protocol were extensive architectural provisions, ranging from broad statements such as "The two parties are equally committed to preserve and protect the historic character of the city in a way which does not harm or change that character in any part of the city"[29] to precise details including the reopening of Shuhada Street, a former Palestinian commercial area closed by the Israelis, within four months. Twenty years later, the street remains closed to vehicles and Palestinians, except those living in the residential areas beyond. The itemization of such terms in the Hebron Protocol makes clear that the battle for control of cities in the West Bank was being fought explicitly within the realm of architecture and planning, deploying the tools and techniques of the discipline for military goals.

29 Israel Ministry of Foreign Affairs, "Protocol Concerning the Redeployment in Hebron," *Israel Ministry of Foreign Affairs*, January 17, 1997, goo.gl/cUF1J5.

Palestinian efforts to control territory within Hebron similarly instrumentalized the procedures and language of architecture and planning. Shortly prior to the signing of the Hebron Protocol, the Hebron Rehabilitation Committee (HRC) was created in August 1996 by presidential decree with three main goals that make explicit the connection in their work between architectural preservation and the construction of a Palestinian political future. The HRC's work has been funded by international development aid, including multiple project partnerships with the United Nations Development Programme (UNDP). In contrast to Israeli settlements, where construction is the most common architectural mode deployed for political gains, the Palestinian political establishment in Hebron has instead used historical preservation techniques as their sociospatial tool of choice. Their battle is to preserve what remains of the architectural, and thus sociopolitical, Palestinian heritage in the West Bank.

According to their website, the HRC has the following main objectives:

1. Preserve the cultural heritage by maintaining the constitutional elements of old buildings, as well as preserving the whole urban fabric.

2. Revive the Old City by consolidating ties with the population, reusing abandoned buildings, upgrading the infrastructure, and connecting the Old City to the city's other parts.

3. Counter and limit Israeli settlements inside the Old City by surrounding settlements with inhabited buildings to prevent their horizontal expansion; and to avert the urban interconnection of these settlements by increasing Arab demographic density between them.[30]

30 "About HRC," *Hebron Rehabilitation Committee*, published January 1, 2011, goo.gl/Fm2olK.

The HRC's stated goals make clear the link between the restoration of historical architecture, preservation of Hebron's Old City, and combating the Israeli settlements within Hebron by increasing the density of Palestinian use and occupation. Just as Israeli settlement architecture contributes to the aim of an expanded Israeli nation, Palestinian architectural preservation and rehabilitation efforts in Hebron instrumentalize the built environment in service of their political efforts to construct a nation in disputed territory. In both cases, these built realities are prefigurative attempts to construct a not-yet-actual state and are made possible by aid. The

A checkpoint at the entrance to Shuhada Street

This plaza was renovated with funding from the Hebron Rehabilitation Committee, a Palestinian architectural and cultural preservation group.

ephemeral and as-yet-illusory nation-states battling for dominance and international recognition in the West Bank are both the products of humanitarian aid, populated by humanitarian subjects.

The HRC's rehabilitation efforts in Hebron's Old City have garnered recognition in the architectural discipline as well as within political and development aid circles. The HRC's rehabilitation work won an Aga Khan Award for Architecture in 1998[31] (the jury included Fredric Jameson and Zaha Hadid, among others) and went on to win the Yasser Arafat Prize for Achievement in 2008 and the UN World Habitat Award in 2013. The HRC's ongoing rehabilitation and preservation work has been made possible by the generous contributions of donor states through the UNDP, including in recent years the Arab Fund for Economic and Social Development, the Catalan Agency for Development Cooperation, the Swedish International Development Cooperation Agency, the government of Germany, and the Spanish Agency for International Development Cooperation, among others.[32]

31 The Aga Khan Award for Architecture Master Jury Statement from the 1996–98 cycle reads in part, "The Hebron Conservation effort as well as the Indore Slum networking project were considered exceptional in ways that are a departure from the conventional approach to upgrading. Both shared the idea of reclaiming community space from growing social and physical environmental degradation. In the case of Hebron, the project was initiated and managed by a community under siege." "The Master Jury Statement," *AKDN*, goo.gl/1oY4FY.

32 "The Annual Report – 2008," *Hebron Rehabilitation Committee*, published January 1, 2011, goo.gl/rOUs66.

Worshippers Way

After an ambush in early November 2002, when twelve Israelis were killed by Palestinian sniper fire between the settlement of Kiryat Arba and the Cave of the Patriarchs in the Old City of Hebron, the Israeli government publicly supported the demolition of a large swath of a Palestinian neighborhood in Hebron for the construction of a new road linking Kiryat Arba to the Cave of the Patriarchs, ostensibly for security reasons. However, this response to a single incident of violence with a large-scale urban planning response must be examined more closely in order to appreciate the full scale of urban effects caused by the demolition, beyond the creation of a new road. According to an article published by *Ha'aretz* in the aftermath of the attack, "Prime Minister Ariel Sharon told IDF commanders in Hebron on Sunday that the opportunity that now presents itself in the wake of the attack Friday evening in the city, in which twelve Israelis were killed, must be exploited to establish new facts on the ground. Israel Radio reported that Sharon said that territorial continuity between the settlement of Kiryat Arba and the Jewish section of Hebron, including the Tomb of the Patriarchs, must be ensured."[33] The creation of such "territorial continuity" was then accomplished by Decree Number 61/02/T to Expropriate Property, issued by the IDF on November 29, barely two weeks after the Hebron ambush attack. The IDF's military decree for demolitions in Hebron was used as a dual tool of urban planning and counterterrorism operations, exemplifying a strategy described by Stephen Graham, Marshall Berman, and others as "urbicide," the deliberate destruction of a city for political or military reasons. The

Following an ambush in 2002 that killed twelve Israelis, the Israeli government authorized the demolition of a group of Palestinian houses to create a secure "prayer road" connecting the settlement of Kiryat Arba to the Cave of the Patriarchs, known as the Ibrahimi Mosque to Palestinians.

Hebron ambush and the IDF's military urbanist response occurred in the wake of Operation Defensive Shield, a series of coordinated military attacks in major Palestinian cities during which 140 multifamily housing blocks were destroyed and 1,500 were damaged, leaving 4,000 people homeless. While the largest military offensive was carried out in Jenin, Hebron also suffered substantial demolitions during the operation.[34]

33 Gidon Alon, Aluf Benn, and Ha' Ha'aretz Service, "PM Calls for Territorial Continuity from Kiryat Arba to Hebron," *Ha'aretz*, November 17, 2002, goo.gl/cWrSdR.

34 Stephen Graham, *Cities Under Siege: The New Military Urbanism* (London: Verso, 2011), 226.

The edge of the Israeli settlement Kiryat Arba, across the valley from the Palestinian city of Hebron

After Decree Number 61/02/T, a petition was then submitted on December 11 to the High Court of Justice on behalf of the Hebron municipality, in which Hebron's residents and the HRC argued that the decree required the demolition of twenty-two buildings with historical and architectural significance. The petition included a statement from architect Shmuel Groag of Bimkom – Planners for Planning Rights, a nonprofit organization, stating that the proposed route of the promenade "severely damages cultural, historical, archaeological, and architectural values, together with severe damage to the quality of life of the residents of the Jabber neighborhood who live there and those who have been forced to leave."[35] We walked this route during one of our visits to Hebron, through the Ibrahimi Mosque checkpoint and uphill passing the Cave of the Patriarchs, surrounded by watchtowers and cameras onto Worshippers Way, cutting through the Palestinian neighborhood demolished by IDF decree to create a clear path for the route up to Kiryat Arba. The street itself was well paved and little used, with no traffic apart from a few Palestinian kids playing in the street and one Israeli settler family passing by in a car. Our companions along the route were mainly IDF soldiers, who leaned against their guard posts directing looks of intense boredom at the scenery and the passersby in equal measure.

35 Esther Zandberg, "Pernicious Promenade," *Ha'aretz*, December 12, 2002, goo.gl/RTKxBG.

Along the length of Worshippers Way from the Cave of the Patriarchs to Kiryat Arba, we passed through an array of the technologies which orchestrate and control the separation of territories and populations in the West Bank: checkpoints with metal detectors and turnstiles, large concrete barrier walls, low wood and barbed wire barricades, video cameras mounted to existing buildings, watchtowers with armed guards atop residential roofs, roving military patrols on foot. These are the tools which enable the maintenance and modulation of the level of violence applied to humanitarian space.

The Green Line and the Barrier Wall, Technologies of Separation

Humanitarian aid sustains persistently temporary occupations and displacements, and produces humanitarian spaces that enable the conditions of both the settlers and the Palestinians to endure through technologies of separation. These technologies enable a permanent instability, thereby justifying continuing international support, which contributes further to the practices and spatial products that prolong that unstable condition, just as the militarization of areas outside the Green Line is justified by the need for mutual security in the absence of a permanent boundary, even as it undermines chances for a lasting peace. The manipulation of the temporal dimension of a crisis is one aspect of the affinity between humanitarian aid and security interests, and of the architecture and spatial configurations produced by their convergence.

The Green Line necessarily operates ideologically more than physically, as a conceptually absolute separation of the warring parties. In 2002 the Israeli government initiated a plan to construct a physical analogue to the Green Line, a barrier—known variously as the "apartheid wall," "security fence," "separation barrier," or "seam zone"—to separate Jerusalem from the West Bank. While they follow different paths, the Green Line prefigures the barrier as a built reality, an image of perfect division, though one rendered in a surprisingly heterogeneous range of shapes and materials—concrete slabs, trenches, barbed wire, metal fencing, visual surveillance, checkpoints, observation towers, and patrol roads.

In practice, the separation barrier is a far subtler and more flexible device than the images of its eight-meter-tall concrete slabs would suggest. The common image of the wall as a concrete edifice is in reality only about 10 percent of its total length. Most of the barrier is a 60–100 meter no-man's-land girded by three layers of barbed wire fencing and trenches to prevent vehicles from passing, hypothetically reconfigurable according to tactical necessities. The barrier is more mutable than the Green Line precisely because it is purely physical; unlike the Green Line, its reality is assumed.

In fact, large portions of the barrier have not been built, and construction has slowed since 2007, owing to improving relations between Israel and the Palestinian National Authority. The discontinuity of the barrier reveals a disjunction between its justifications and its effects: while it falls short of safeguarding Israel's territory from attack, it effectively disrupts the spatial continuity of the Palestinian areas caught between the barrier and the Green Line and obstructs Palestinians workers who legally cross daily for work. At Checkpoint 300, the entrance in the wall between Jerusalem and Bethlehem, hundreds of Palestinian workers line up daily at 4 a.m., often waiting hours to pass through.

The Green Line is most effective and consequential not in spite of, but through its discrepancies with the physical conditions on the ground, making the most of the gap between ideological separation and the compromises of physical space. The advantages of an immaterial construction such as the Green Line over a physical wall were not missed by Ariel Sharon, whose Likud Party initially opposed the construction of the barrier, in part because it embodied the two-state solution, and also because it meant formalizing territorial concessions to the Palestinians. The physicality of the wall was seen by Sharon as too final, limiting the framework of future negotiations, relinquishing claims to the whole of the Land of Israel, and delineating the spatial strategy of the settlements.

The wall was the central focus of the International Court of Justice hearings that occurred in 2003, wherein all discussions of humanitarian issues and human rights violations were framed through their engagement with the physical form. The power and effects of the architecture were the focus of debate—was it an apparatus of security or violence, an aggressive or defensive form? Thousands of pages describing the wall and its gates and their openings and closures, extensive documentation of site visits and interviews, along with the written opinions of forty-eight countries explored the humanitarian crisis through the form of the wall as it impacted the Palestinian right to self-determination. These legal proceedings illustrate the political life of the wall and its existence in diplomatic as well as physical space. As Eyal Weizman has observed, it was the architecture itself that was on trial, with all issues of sovereignty and violence, terrorism and statehood framed through interactions with a single wall.

The wall is defined by the Palestinian written opinion as "the integrated system of concrete walls, fences (including electric fences), barriers, barbed wire zones, ditches, trenches, trace paths, patrol roads, and fortified guard towers being built by Israel in the Occupied Palestinian Territory."[36] The documents submitted by the Palestinians include extensive visual documentation of the wall through photographs and maps, a spatial catalogue of the wall which framed each act of violence through its architectural manifestations.

36 International Court of Justice (ICJ), case, Legal Consequences of the Construction of a Wall in the Occupied Palestinian Territory, "Written Statement submitted by Palestine," January 29, 2004, 17, goo.gl/LUyWsA.

The Israeli statement essentially ignores the physical reality of the wall, instead centering on the terrorist threat posed by Palestine, and thereby framing the wall as a necessary and temporary architecture of crisis. The Israeli written statement devotes only two pages to addressing the physical wall and the remaining 244 pages to the issues of security and terrorist threats.[37] The Israeli opinion is prefaced by a letter from the Deputy Director General and legal advisor of the Ministry of Foreign Affairs, written in a tenor which imbues the formal submission on the wall with an air of urgency and frames the architecture as a temporary security measure. The Director's letter reads, "as these words are being written, news has just broken of yet another terrorist atrocity on a public bus in Jerusalem only a few kilometers from this office. In these first few minutes, the news is that ten people have been killed and a further forty-five injured. It seems likely that the numbers of dead and injured will increase in the next hours as the news becomes clearer. The television images of the scene are deeply distressing." The reader is intended to perceive the wall as an architecture of necessity operating under dire circumstances. The Israeli statement on the wall uses a language of immediate emergency which excuses its built forms and justifies the social consequences.

37 ICJ, case, Legal Consequences of the Construction of a Wall in the Occupied Palestinian Territory, "Letter dated 29 January 2004 from the Deputy Director General and Legal Advisor of the Ministry of Foreign Affairs, together with the Written Statement of the Government of Israel," January 30, 2004, goo.gl/Q00el0.

In the course of the proceedings, Israel submitted the written opinion that human rights laws were not applicable in the Occupied Territories. As summarized by the Security Council, "Israel denies that the International Covenant on Civil and Political Rights and the International Covenant on Economic, Social and Cultural Rights, both of which it has signed, are applicable to the occupied Palestinian territory. It asserts that humanitarian law is the protection granted in a conflict situation such as the one in the West Bank and Gaza Strip, whereas human rights treaties were intended for the protection of citizens from their own Government in times of peace."[38]

38 ICJ, "Summary of the Advisory Opinion of 9 July 2004," (see note 21).

Though rejected by the Security Council, this bold claim reveals an important relationship between the humanitarian subject and the State. The Israeli submission stated that the granting of human rights inherently implies a relationship between the subject and state akin to that of citizenship, whereas Palestinians in the Occupied Palestinian Territories were mere humanitarian subjects.[39] Despite the 2004 ruling of the International Court of Justice, the wall continues to move forward in a state of continual expansion and revision. It is a mechanism for defining national boundaries which refuses constraint, a mobile and transitory apparatus which refuses to contain that which it encircles.

39 Ibid.

Gates

In its gaps and checkpoints, the wall functions as more of a permeable membrane than an absolute division, channeling and regulating the movement of people and goods across its length. Rather than separating completely, it instead orchestrates the points of access between the two sides through a series of controlled gates. Five major barrier crossings exist along the wall, all but one erected at places where the wall crosses the invisible boundary of the Green Line,[40] the promised future border of the Palestinian State.

40 David Newman, "The Renaissance of a Border That Never Died," in *Borderlines and Borderlands*, ed. Alexander C. Diener and Joshua Hagen (London: Rowan and Littlefield Publishers, 2010), 98.

A series of videos shot by B'Tselem, an Israeli human rights organization, reveal the banality of the barrier's oppression: we observe the banter between Israeli soldiers and Palestinians waiting to be processed, who know they'll be back the next day waiting in the same long lines, the men half-heartedly running from the border patrol, who explain to the camera that they run so that they won't miss dinner by being detained, the arguments between Israeli soldiers about whether the Palestinian workers can be allowed through one gate or need travel down the road to the next.[41] The logic of the walls, gates, and towers structures the lives of the men and women in the videos, both Palestinian and Israeli, as inhabitants of humanitarian space.

41 B'Tselem, "Catch Me," March 1, 2011, goo.gl/wMeKaX.

The presence of IDF troops known as "humanitarian officers" at many of the gates is indicative of the suspect uses of supposedly benevolent aid. Apparently employed to provide care to border crossers, in particular the sick and elderly, the humanitarian officers' role reveals the operating logic of the gates in the checkpoint system. Humanitarian officers act as carefully calibrated valves on a humanitarian situation that, as Adi Ophir has written, is maintained indefinitely at the subcrisis level. The suspension of the catastrophe through humanitarian aid has become part of the machinery of the occupation.[42] Gates,

Checkpoint 300 near Rachel's Tomb crossing the barrier wall, outside Bethlehem. The checkpoint has a "humanitarian lane," which is required by international law and is intended to expedite the passage of the elderly, women, children, and the infirm.

whether those at the barrier crossing or at the Red Crescent distribution points in Dheisheh, are a means of controlling the threshold of the crisis by organizing the circulation of bodies and goods, maintaining allowable degrees of violence and insecurity rather than seeking to eliminate them entirely.

42 Adi Ophir, "The Politics of Catastrophization," in *Contemporary States of Emergency: The Politics of Military and Humanitarian Interventions*, ed. Didier Fassin and Maria Pandolfi (New York: Zone Books, 2010), 81.

Parks

One of the latest sections of the wall to be built is around the E-1 area to the East of Jerusalem. The proposed wall would encircle Ma'ale Adumim, a settlement whose strategic position between Jerusalem and the West Bank is critical for the peace process and the potential of a future Palestinian state. While the Green Line exacerbates the crisis in the immediate present, continually justifying its existence with a promise of a future resolution, the proposed physical wall around Ma'ale Adumim is an annexation of Palestinian territory without concession or apology.

Positioned at a critical location between Jerusalem and the deserts of the West Bank, Ma'ale Adumim is home to 35,000 residents and yet is not legally a part of Israel. It is a city in the form of a tower, its streets and infrastructure hugging the slopes and its houses oriented in concentric rings, staggered to provide the maximum views of the landscape.

Ma'ale Adumim was originally set aside in 1967 as the site of a future industrial park, an economic haven that would cater to businesses in Jerusalem with lower labor costs and financial incentives to encourage economic development. The industrial park still operates today as Mishor Adumim Industrial Park, though 35,000 other residents also occupy the land. It was not until 1991 that the tens of thousands of residents in Ma'ale Adumim were declared to be living in a municipality rather than a massive industrial park. The retroactive declaration of urban form removed an element of intent from the construction by describing a reality rather than an ambition. Ma'ale Adumim was naturalized through its gradual transition from foreign territory to industrial park to city.

This semantic camouflage was used to formally justify all kinds of development in the name of economic growth, a range of construction types and programs that had little connection (if any) to the purpose of the industrial park. It was only after the city had established itself for decades that it could be declared to exist.

Commercial advertisements for the Adumim Industrial Park describe its benefits as "close proximity to all places in Israel," a "peaceful desert atmosphere," excellent security and a well-established infrastructure.[43] Security and commercial opportunities are discussed in smooth real estate hyperbole, with diagrams of transit speed and tax cuts in the background of the image. Political realities and national boundaries are ignored in the glowing descriptions of access to infrastructure whose existence is in direct contravention to international law. Footage of cars and trucks traveling along Israeli highways punctuate the video, reinforcing the overall emphasis on infrastructure and connection to the state (and market) of Israel. As both a city and an industrial park, Ma'ale Adumim uses the rhetoric of security and efficiency in its construction and physical organization in a tone that blends upbeat capitalism with paranoid militarism.

43 Videos produced by The Nature of Things for the Ma'Ale Adumim Economic & Development Company in 2002, goo.gl/dm1E37.

The numerous areas administered by the Israeli national nature preserve program in the West Bank are another type of park urbanism. Israel currently designates forty-eight areas as nature reserves in the West Bank, about 5 percent of the land in the Occupied Palestinian Territories. Much of this area is concentrated in Area C, a region under the authority of the Israeli military. The nature preserves contribute to the fragmentation of the Palestinian territory: Palestinian herders can be fined for trespassing on the nature preserve, and structures built by Palestinians on the land have been demolished by the IDF.[44] At the same time, at least four Israeli outposts constructed on nature reserves have been allowed to remain, a fact confirmed by the Israeli Nature and Parks Authority.[45] These parks are part of the strategy of flexible spatial occupation of the West Bank, allowing areas to be brought under control by the occupying authority under the premise of scientific environmentalism.

44 Yuval Azoulay, "Palestinian Herders Fined for Trespassing West Bank Nature Preserve," *Ha'aretz*, February 22, 2010, goo.gl/Gxwjxn.

45 Zafrir Rinat, "Outposts Blossom in W. Bank Nature Reserves," *Ha'aretz*, January 16, 2004, goo.gl/ZLyOLp.

Imaging and Intelligibility

In the West Bank, the principles of the gate—the continuous modulation of circulation by degrees—operate at the level of the image as well. The planimetric image of the West Bank is a subtly controlled spatial visualization produced through satellite imaging. The satellite image, an instrument of ubiquitous global vision readily available on laptops around the world, is a means of representation as vulnerable to manipulation as the pencil or brush, with less obvious traces and thus less readily apparent motivations. What is at stake in these images is the knowledge of real spaces, territories, and communities.

The rules that govern the production and distribution of such satellite images are termed *shutter policies*, governmental regulations dictating the methodology and quality of image gathering within their territories by private companies such as DigitalGlobe, Space Imaging, or GeoEye. In the case of Israel, the commercial availability of satellite images is constrained by an amendment added to the 1997 US National Defense Authorization Act, a clause titled "Prohibition on Collection and Release of Detailed Satellite Imagery Relating to Israel."[46] Known as the Kyl-Bingaman Amendment, the law calls for a federal agency, the National Oceanic and Aeronautical Association (NOAA) Commercial Remote Sensing Regulatory Affairs, to limit the commercial distribution of high resolution images of Israel by preventing US-based imaging companies from photographing and disseminating images of Israel and the Occupied Palestinian Territories. Until 2012, with the launch of the Göktürk Satellite by Turkey, all commercial satellite imaging providers were either US-based or complied with similar shutter policies regarding images of Israel. Even today, the amendment remains in effect, and pertains to all non-military satellite images produced or distributed by US companies, such as those available on Google Earth and Google Maps. Two meters of ground per pixel renders the West Bank fuzzy, and visual control of the landscape thereby remains in the hands of the Israeli government.

46 In the US, the Kyl-Bingaman Amendment to the 1997 National Defense Authorization Act (NDAA) prohibits US-based commercial satellite companies from obtaining and distributing high-resolution images of Israel and the Occupied Palestinian Territories. The company Space Imaging had to lower the resolution from its IKONOS satellite from 1-meter resolution to 2-meters resolution. Google Earth sources its images from US-based companies that are subject to the Kyl-Bingaman Amendment. Full text of the 1997 NDAA, goo.gl/yHnCbg.

An image that seems to make objective disclosures has the power to hide things in plain view. Many phenomena, objects, and events will remain undetectable, even at the best resolution allowable under the shutter policies. A human body does not register at this scale, creating a lifeless image of the camps, settlements, and territories. We cannot clearly see the digging of new foundations for a settlement, nor the footpaths of Palestinians crossing the border for work each day. We are unable to decipher the organization of the refugee camps, so dense that their internal logic disappears through the representational regime imposed by Israel and allied nations.

The controlled fuzziness of low-resolution satellite images is a representational technique whose physical analogue is the gate. Rather than prohibiting access to the image absolutely, as in the blackout strategies of more primitive forms of censorship, resolution control establishes a threshold of visibility and regulates the conditions of the image's circulation. Everyone can see it, but some see more than others, according to degrees of visibility that may not be readily apparent. The omission of these subtler realities of the built environment from satellite imaging renders them all the more important. Control of representation and the resolution of the landscape allows for acts of architecture to be committed unseen. Humanitarian space may aspire to be a moral sphere that transcends politics, but it is still produces and is governed by regimes of intelligibility.

TERRITORIES

West Bank

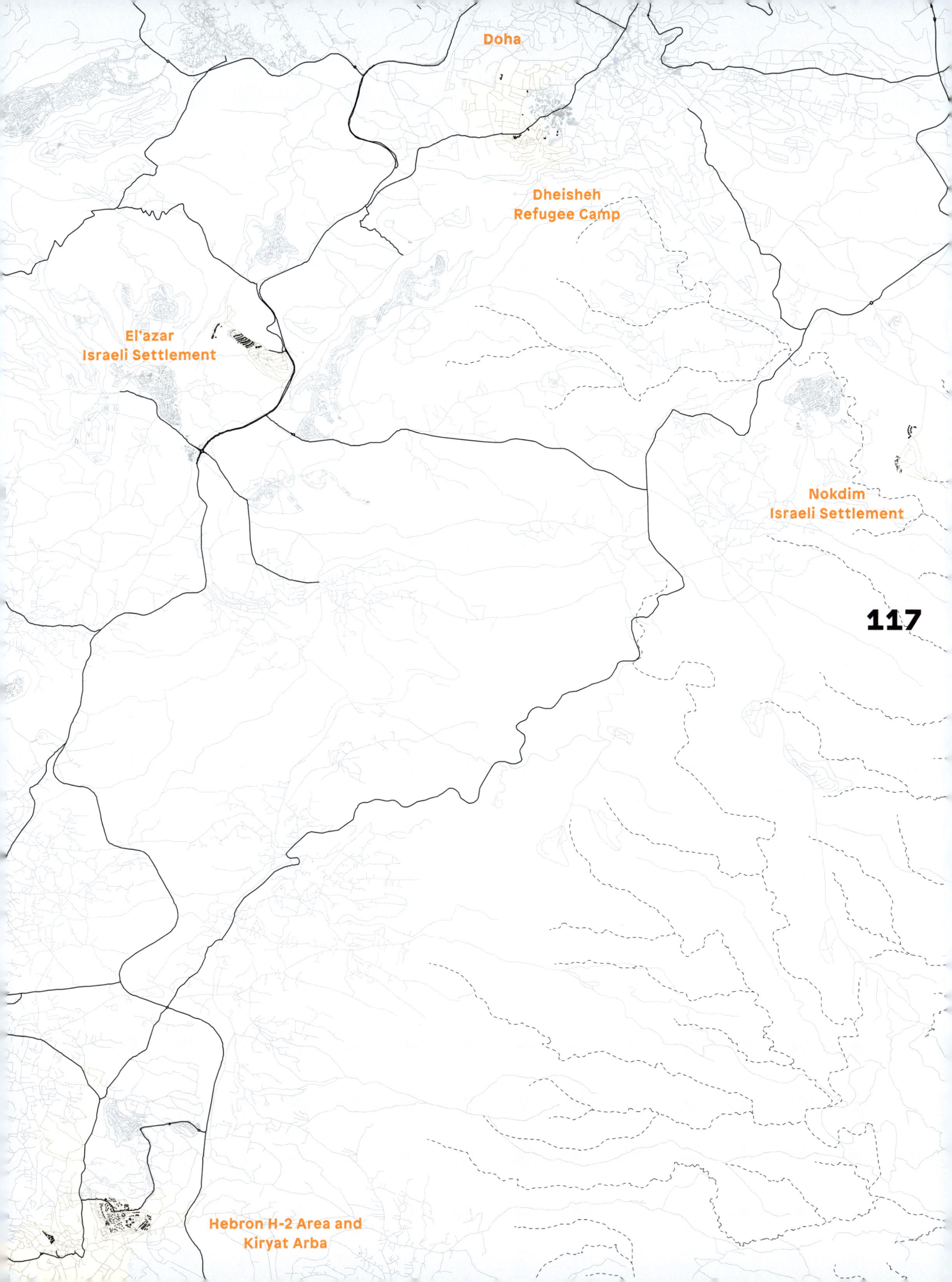
Doha
Dheisheh
Refugee Camp
El'azar
Israeli Settlement
Nokdim
Israeli Settlement
Hebron H-2 Area and
Kiryat Arba

Dheisheh Refugee Camp

Dheisheh was the first Palestinian refugee camp to open, following the 1948 Arab-Israeli war. Today it has a population of more than 13,000 people.

1

UNRWA Dheisheh Girls School

UNRWA administers the Dheisheh Girls School, a primary school.

2003.12.28

2016.07.22

2

UNRWA Health Clinic

UNRWA runs a health clinic and aid distribution point in Dheisheh and also serves the surrounding area with primary care and infant health services.

2011.10.20

2016.07.22

3

Red Crescent (ICRC)

The Red Crescent center is a joint project of the Qatari Red Crescent and the German Red Cross to provide relief aid in the camp.

2003.12.28

2013.08.10

2016.07.22

4

Al-Feniq Cultural Center

The center is home to Campus in Camps, an educational program founded by architects Sandi Hilal and Alessandro Petti.

2003.12.28

2016.07.22

5

Helicopter landing pad

The Palestinian National Authority maintains a helipad at the top of the hill on which Dheisheh is built.

2003.12.28

2016.07.22

Doha

Doha is a Palestinian residential area across from the Dheisheh refugee camp and south of Bethlehem. The town has a population of about 10,000 people, many of whom come from families that were previously housed in Dheisheh.

1

Al Amal Kindergarten

The Al Amal Kindergarten is run by a charitable foundation.

2003.12.28

2009.08.05

2016.07.22

2

Ad Doha Girls High School

Constructed in 2009, the school was built with development aid from Amman, Jordan.

2007.11.25

2016.07.22

3

Al Khulafa' Ar Rashideen Girls Elementary School

Construction was funded by the Japanese government with funding for additional floors donated by Catholic Relief Services.

2003.12.28

2009.08.05

2016.07.22

El’azar Israeli Settlement

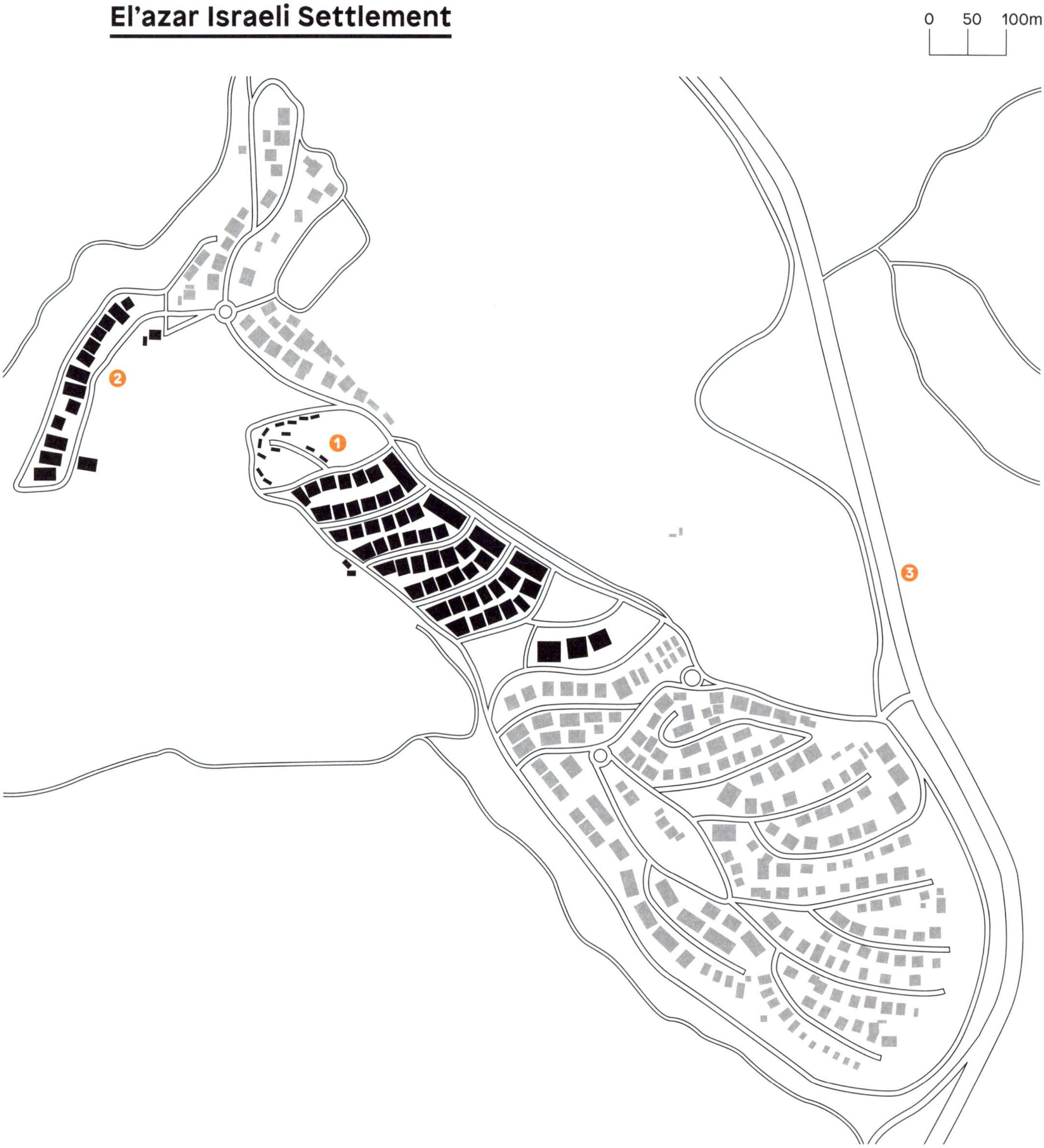

El’azar is a settlement in the Etzion Bloc with a population of about 2,500 people located south of Bethlehem. It was founded in 1975.

1

Settlement Expansion (2012)

This area of El'azar was expanded in 2012.

2002.06.10

2009.08.05

2010.07.14

2011.03.29

2016.06.11

2

Settlement Expansion (2015)

The settlement was expanded again in 2015.

2006.05.13

2011.03.29

2014.09.21

2016.06.11

3

Highway 60 (Israeli road)

Highway 60, also known as the Way of the Patriarchs, connects Jerusalem to settlements and Palestinian cities in the West Bank. Before the Oslo Accords, Palestinians could travel freely on Highway 60, but today, Israel administers checkpoints at sections of the highway that enter into Palestinian National Authority-controlled areas, and additional routes connecting to the highway, bypass roads, have been added to allow Israeli travelers to bypass Palestinian areas, effectively creating separate circulation systems for Palestinians and Israelis. The section of Highway 60 between Jerusalem and the Etzion Bloc is known as the Tunnels Highway due to long stretches that are built underground to bypass the Palestinian city of Bethlehem.

2006.05.13

2016.07.22

Nokdim Israeli Settlement

Nokdim is a settlement in the Judean Hills, part of the Etzion Bloc, and founded in 1982. According to the Israeli NGO Peace Now, about 30 percent of the settlement is built on land that was privately owned by Palestinians, making it an illegal settlement under Israeli law (all of the West Bank settlements are considered illegal under international law). Nokdim is home to Avigdor Lieberman, a prominent right-wing Israeli politician and currently the defense minister. The bypass road leading to Nokdim is informally known as the Lieberman Highway.

1 Settlement expansion area (2012)

Additional homes were built on the north side of the settlement in 2012.

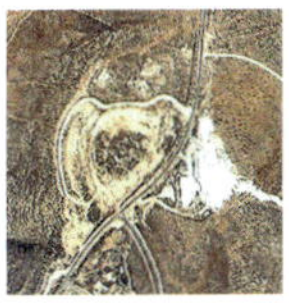
2006.05.13

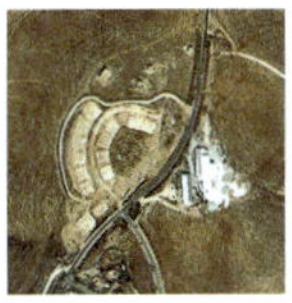
2011.10.20

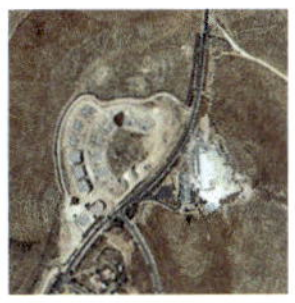
2013.08.10

2016.06.14

2 Bus stop

Like most settlements, Nokdim is easily reached by a network of bus lines that carry passengers from Jerusalem throughout the West Bank.

2006.05.13

2016.06.14

3 Trailer area

On the edge of Nokdim, an area of mobile trailers has been in place for more than a decade, and has slowly expanded by adding more units in recent years.

2007.11.25

2011.10.20

2013.08.13

2016.06.14

Hebron H-2 Area and Kiryat Arba

With a population of around 200,000, the city of Hebron, Al-Khalil in Arabic, is the second-largest city in the West Bank. It is located south of Jerusalem and the Etzion Bloc of settlements. The Old City of Hebron is a site of contention between Israelis and Palestinians, as Israelis have been trying to set up settlements in the densely populated area since the late 1970s. The Ibrahimi Mosque, which is also the site of the Cave of the Patriarchs in the Jewish tradition, was divided into Muslim and Jewish areas after a 1994 attack in which an Israeli settler opened fire in the mosque, killing twenty-nine Palestinians.

1

Kiryat Arba settlement

The settlement Kiryat Arba is in the Judean Hills, separated from Hebron by a valley and olive grove. It was established in 1968, shortly after the Six-Day War, and today has a population of around 7,000. The settlement was intended to reestablish a Jewish presence in Hebron, following a 1929 attack in which sixty-seven Jews were killed by Palestinians, which resulted in the evacuation of the remaining Jewish population.

2006.05.13

2014.10.20

2

Shuhada Street closure

Israel closed Shuhada Street to Palestinians in 1994, following a riot in the area after the Ibrahimi Mosque Massacre.

2011.03.29

2014.10.20

3

Worshippers Way

Worshippers Way is a road that links Kiryat Arba to the Cave of the Patriarchs, known as the Ibrahimi Mosque to Muslims. The road was built following an attack near the settlement in 2002, in which twelve soldiers and guards were killed. To construct the road, Israel expropriated a number of Palestinian-owned buildings and demolished them to clear a path for the road.

2004.02.07

2014.10.20

4

Beit Hadassah settlement

The building was originally a Jewish hospital founded in the late nineteenth century. In 1979 a group of settlers reoccupied the building to create a foothold for Jewish resettlement in the city center of Hebron, which has led to protracted conflict with Palestinians.

2014.10.20

5

Beit Romano settlement

Beit Romano is another Israeli settlement within the historic center of Hebron. The building was constructed in the early twentieth century as a yeshiva, and was reoccupied by Israelis in 1982.

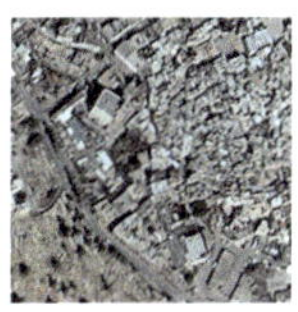
2014.10.20

6

Ibrahimi Mosque checkpoint

The checkpoint near the Ibrahimi Mosque controls foot traffic between the Old City of Hebron and the Cave of the Patriarchs, a contested site that has religious significance to both Jews and Muslims.

2004.02.07

2014.10.20

WEST BANK

Settlement Growth

Despite a few brief freezes in settlement construction during Israeli-Palestinian peace talks, the building and expansion of Israeli settlements in the West Bank has largely continued apace throughout the past two decades, aided in part by international charities that fund and support the settlements, and indirectly through the official development assistance given by the United States to the government of Israel. An analysis of aerial photography provided by the Israeli NGO Peace Now shows the expanding footprints of settlements in areas around East Jerusalem and the West Bank in the years 1997 to 2014. In each period, new houses and infrastructure are added to the settlements, further entrenching this illegal urbanism in the contested territories.

Beitar Illit

1997

1999

2001

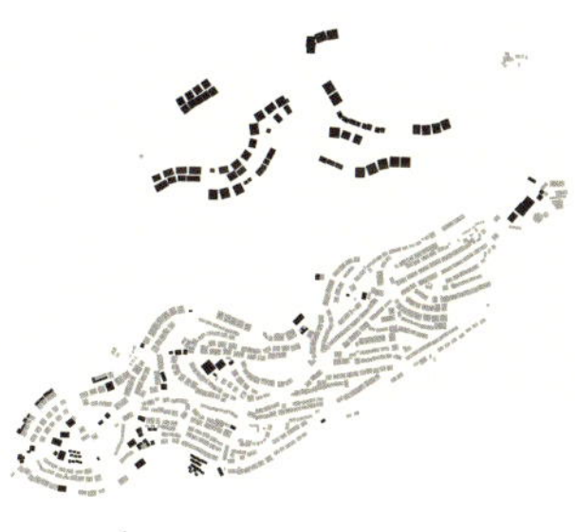

2006

2009

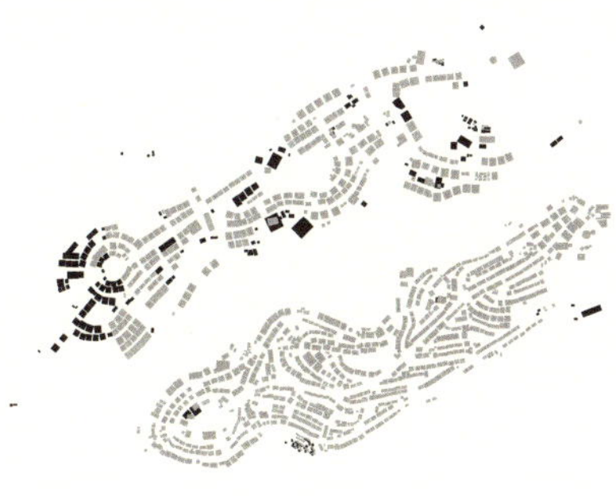

2014

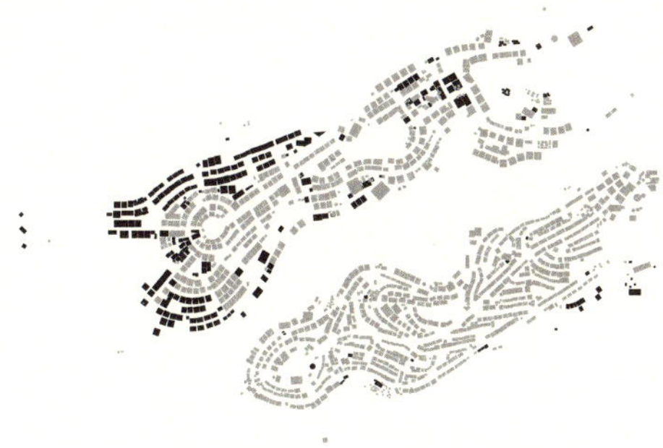

Beitar Illit is part of the Etzion settlement bloc located along Highway 60 south of Jerusalem. It is one of the fastest growing settlements, with a current population of around 50,000 people. Its construction began in the mid-1980s after settler families seized land that previously belonged to the Palestinian village of Husan.

Bruchin

1997

1999

2001

2006

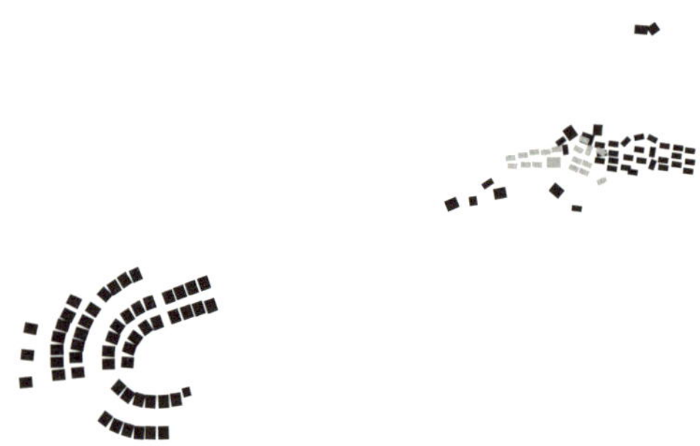

2009

2014

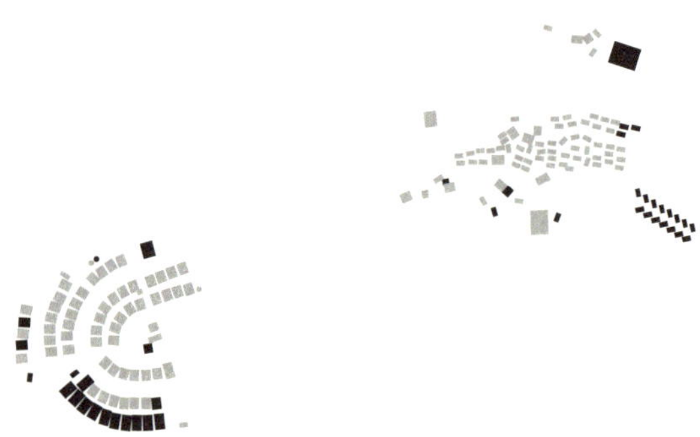

Bruchin was one of three Israeli settlements in the West Bank that were retroactively legalized in 2012. Legalization sparked a building boom in Bruchin, doubling the settlement's size by 2015. Although it is still a small settlement, it has a waiting list of about 100 families as of 2015.

Efrat

1997

1999

2001

2006

2009

2014

Efrat is a large settlement of nearly 10,000 residents. Located south of Jerusalem, it is the unofficial capital of the Etzion block settlements. Efrat is on the eastern side of the main north-south route, Highway 60, which places it on the Palestinian side of the line drawn by the Geneva Initiative, a high level international working group that drew up a proposal for a two-state solution in 2003. Around 1,100 new units were slated for construction in Efrat as of 2015.

Eli

1997

1999

2001

2006

2009

2014

Eli was founded in 1984, and is now home to around 4,000 settlers. It includes a yeshiva of around 500 students, as well as a shopping mall and community center, both recently completed. From 1997 to 2015, its footprint doubled in size to around 610 hectares.

Har Homa

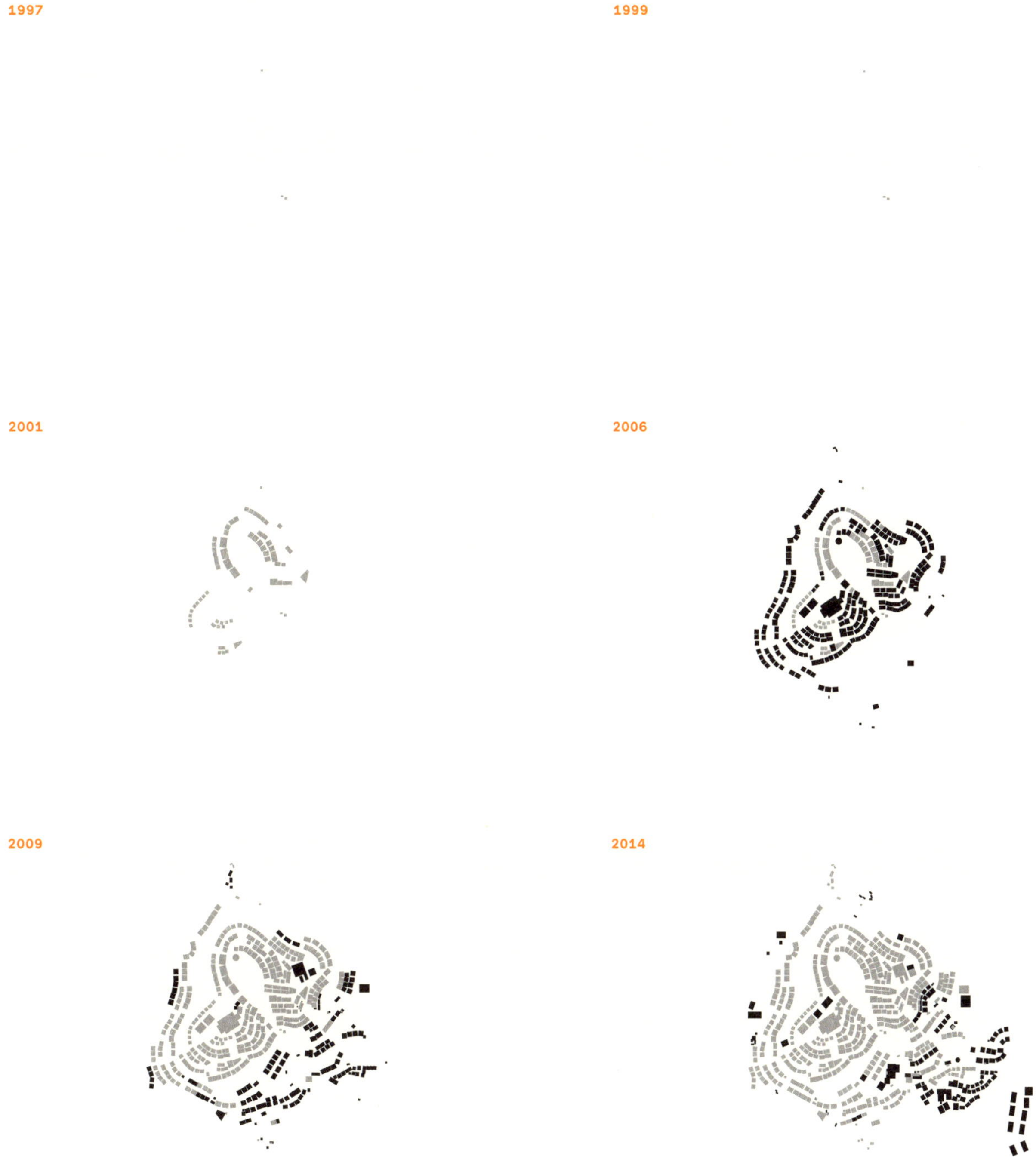

Located between Jerusalem and Bethlehem, Har Homa is a settlement of about 25,000 people. The land on which it is built was expropriated by the Israeli government in 1991, which prompted land-owners, both Palestinian and Israeli, to bring a case to the Israeli Supreme Court. Their appeal was unsuccessful, and construction of settler homes began in the mid-1990s. The construction was met by resolutions introduced in the UN, which were ultimately vetoed by the US. The settlement serves the strategic purpose of constraining the growth of nearby Palestinian towns, and consolidating Israel's claim to the areas around Jerusalem.

Leshem

1997

1999

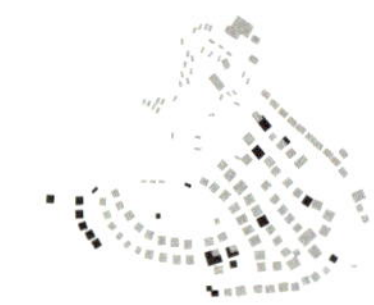

2001

2006

2009

2014

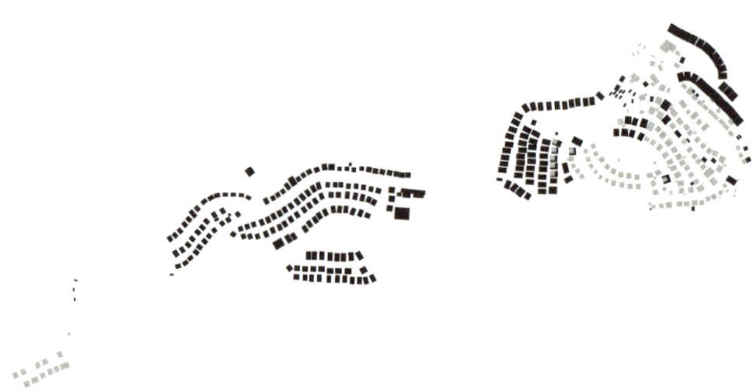

Leshem is a relatively small settlement of a little over 100 families, officially founded in 2013. The Israeli government considers Leshem a new neighborhood of a nearby older settlement, Alei Zahav, but Leshem has its own community council and markets itself as a new community, distinct from its older neighbor. As of 2015, development in Leshem was continuing, with new homes under construction.

Modi'in Illit

1997

1999

2001

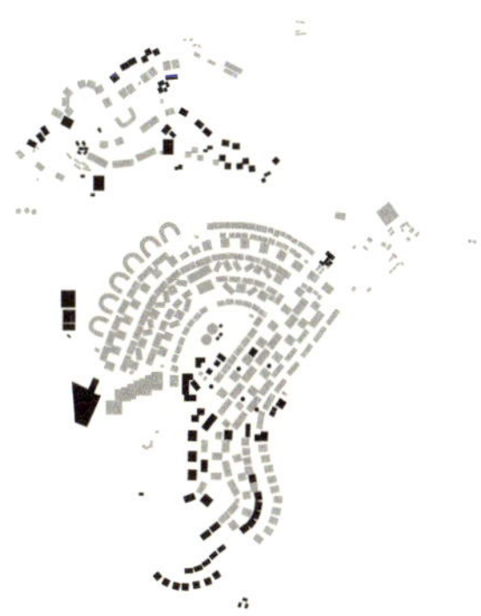

2006

2009

2014

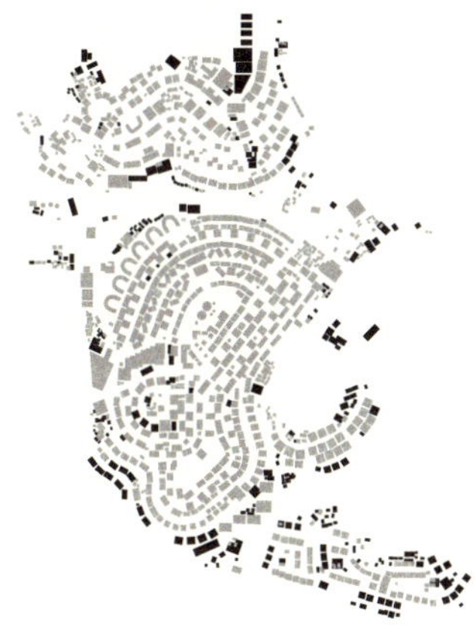

Modi'in Illit is a large and fast growing settlement just outside the 1967 boundaries of Israel, and built on land that formerly comprised five Palestinian villages. Its population of more than 60,000 residents makes it the largest settlement in the area. Although the settlement is considered by most national governments to be outside the legitimate borders of the state of Israel, the path of Israel's West Bank Separation Barrier was designed to enclose Modi'in Illit, signaling that the Israeli government intends for the settlement to remain part of Israel under any possible agreement with the Palestinians on a two-state solution.

Ofra

1997

1999

2001

2006

2009

2014

Ofra is sited northeast of the Palestinian city of Ramallah, and east of the Israeli Separation Barrier. The Israeli government acknowledges that most of Ofra's land was formerly owned by Palestinians, making the settlement illegal not only under international law (like all Israeli settlements), but also under Israeli national law. The development of Ofra began in 1975 without the approval of the government, but it was officially recognized in 1977 after the Likud Party defeated Labor.

4. Nairobi and Humanitarian Government

Humanitarian government has shaped the city of Nairobi. The city is both an international hub for NGOs and UN organizations and a testing ground for their urban development programs sited in the city's slums. Home to the United Nations Office at Nairobi (UNON)—the international headquarters of the UN Human Settlements Programme (UN-Habitat) and the UN Environment Programme (UNEP), and the African regional offices of the UN High Commissioner for Refugees (UNHCR), the UN International Children's Emergency Fund (UNICEF), the UN Development Programme (UNDP), the UN Educational, Scientific and Cultural Organization (UNESCO), the World Health Organization (WHO), the World Food Programme (WFP), the International Monetary Fund (IMF), and the World Bank—the city plays host to a transitory population of diplomats, bureaucrats, and aid workers, while across the city lie some of the most well known slums in the world. Nairobi has been characterized by Kenyan architect and urbanist Alfred Omenya as an example of "island urbanism," an archipelago of disjunctive and mutually exclusive areas separated by walls, where slums abut wealthy suburbs. But the appearance of islands belies a more complicated series of interdependencies between those spaces.[1] Taken together, the slum, the international institutions that administer the various slum upgrading programs, and a range of state and private actors—from the Kenyan government and Nairobi municipal administration to the corporations that market the goods and services required for humanitarian government—constitute a spatiopolitical complex, all parts of which are highly interrelated.

1 Alfred Omenya, "Island Urbanism: Spatial Segregation in Nairobi," in *Learning from Nairobi Mobility*, ed. Köln International School of Design, Goethe-Institute Kenya, University of Nairobi (Cologne: KISD Editions, 2010).

Among the slums of Nairobi, Kibera in particular is a cause célèbre of international NGOs and a laboratory for development policies and humanitarian practices, including most recently a massive construction program of new housing for slum dwellers in areas of Kibera that were cleared in 2009 in order to become sites of reconstruction. Given the heavy presence of international humanitarian aid organizations in Nairobi, it may be surprising that Kibera has existed for as long as it has, seemingly unresponsive to decades of efforts to improve its conditions despite being located in a city that is a center of humanitarian bureaucracy. But Kibera's apparent intransigency is not accidental, nor is it simply an example of the failure of the state welfare programs or development aid efforts. Rather it is the effect of a durable and complex contestation between multiple parties: the residents of Kibera, the landlords who own the overwhelming majority of the slum's structures, national and local governments from the colonial period through independence to today, and, increasingly, the international organizations that hold ever greater influence in Nairobi's politics and urban planning.

The Model Slum

In the world of international aid, discussions of Kibera are both enigmatic and unavoidable. While its boundaries and population figures are contested, Kibera is an extremely well known case study in slum urbanism. Kibera has come to embody the image of the extremes of contemporary urban poverty in the Global South in recent years, with statistics and photographs of its residents deployed as shorthand in discussions ranging from human rights to education, access to water and sanitation, and the role of the "international community" in urban development. Often referred to as the largest slum in Africa, Kibera is foregrounded as a stand-in for slums throughout the world.

Through this elevated profile, Kibera serves as a stage for the performance of humanitarian pledges to Africa, and by extension, to slum dwellers globally. During his first official trip as Secretary-General of the United Nations, Ban Ki-moon toured Kibera with local residents and international media. Assuring the press and other attendees of the UN's continuing commitment to Africa on the whole, he stated, "My presence here in the first month of my tenure as the Secretary-General of the United Nations is a strong sign of the growing partnership between the United Nations and the African Union and the high priority I attach to Africa."[2] Kibera, located just across town from the UN's headquarters for Africa, is intensely studied, highly visible, and subjected to ongoing attempts by the UN and other international actors to find a solution to the "challenge of slums."[3]

2 Ernest Harsch, "Africa a Priority for New UN Head," *Africa Renewal* (Africa Section of the United Nations Department of Public Information) 21, no. 1 (April 2007): 3.

3 United Nations Human Settlements Programme, *The Challenge of Slums: Global Report on Human Settlements 2003* (London: Earthscan Publications, 2003).

Kibera lies in the southwest of Nairobi, bounded by a railroad that runs along part of its northern edge and the Nairobi Dam and the Southern Bypass Road highway to the south. In the 1880s, the area that Kibera now occupies was formally designated a land reserve, separate and semiautonomous from the city of Nairobi, the retirement estate for members of the King's African Rifles, a colonial regiment of Nubian soldiers who had fought on behalf of the British in Africa. The Nubian veterans were granted the right to occupy the territory with their families and to own the homes they inhabited, but they were not allowed to own the land itself, as British policies during colonial rule prevented Africans from holding land property in Nairobi until 1954.[4] The land ownership policy was intended to discourage the permanent settlement of Africans in the city, fearing that urban life would "detribalize" the African population and lead to popular movements against the colonial power. The Nubian soldiers were seen as an exception, given that they had already fought for the colonizing British power. Originally from Sudan, the members of the former battalion were effectively displaced persons in Nairobi, having been temporarily absorbed into the British Empire and then made redundant at the end of the conflict. But they were still, of course, African, and therefore conferred a distinct status in the racially divided colonial city. The Nubians were designated detribalized natives and granted the right to live on 1,600 hectares of land on what was then the outskirts of Nairobi, which they named Kibra, "land of the forest."

4 Mike Davis, *Planet of Slums* (London: Verso, 2006), 51.

The racist land tenure policies of the British administration were designed to prevent Africans from becoming permanent, land-holding residents, with the goal of retaining Nairobi as a city for Europeans involved in the administrative, mercantile, and military operations that constituted British colonialism in Africa. These were urban planning strategies and policies implemented with the intent of disenfranchising Africans, the majority of the population, while allocating them a segregated residential space close to the formal city. Of course, at the same time that these policies sought to exclude Africans from the full benefits of citizenship, the colonial city was entirely dependent on indentured workers from throughout Kenya and other British colonies in Africa, and so it was impossible to completely exclude Africans from the operations and routines of Nairobi. Through the Vagrancy Act of 1922, Kenyan natives and migratory workers from other colonies were segregated to lands reserved for specific ethnic groups on the edges of the city. These "native reserves" mark the beginning of the bureaucratic process through which Kibera, the reserve created for the Nubians, was produced as a model slum. Far from spontaneous or informal, the slum is the direct product of decades of government policy, legal codes, and city planning originally based in racist ideology.

In the decades prior to independence, Kibera remained majority Nubian, and the Nubians developed their own systems of property transfer within the community as a distinct area that was segregated from both the British and the Kenyan populations of Nairobi. Over the years, individual houses were handed down within families from the original soldiers, and newer immigrants were absorbed into the community. Though the residents never held any official land titles, they were nonetheless homeowners in a self-governing polity, a group with a provisional coherence produced in part by their exclusion from the officially recognized city. The community was allowed to continue for nearly a century as a semiautonomous portion of the city, economically integrated and physically adjacent but officially separate.

After independence in 1963, Kibera was criticized by the Kenyan government under Jomo Kenyatta as a remnant of colonial oppression and an unjust allocation of Kenyan lands to an originally Sudanese population. The territory was declared an "unauthorized settlement" in 1963, and its land was then designated as a national forest, restructured and absorbed into the state as public land legally owned by the Kenyan government. The same houses, businesses, and families remained in place, but their legal status in relation to the municipal and national governments was changed; even today, the settlement is not officially recognized by the Kenyan government. The Nubian community was denied recognition by the new postcolonial government, and Kibera was removed from official property maps of Nairobi. Though daily life and routines continued largely unchanged, the former homeowners and landlords were now considered squatters, and their community an illegal occupation of public land—a national forest with almost no trees.

The land on which Kibera sits thus has an exceptional status within the city in its exploiting of this legal loophole. Like all parks, whether natural or industrial, the national-forest-as-slum integrates an alien element of the city, something at once necessary to the city and in certain other ways outside and inadmissible to its logic, or, in Giorgio Agamben's term, an inclusive exclusion. The Nubian land reserve and the slum it currently supports represent a physically, socially, and economically connected area of the city, but one that is nonetheless ideologically incompatible.

Immediately after Kibera was rendered unauthorized, the municipal government also outlawed the building of permanent structures, as the former reserve was now considered a public park. These new building codes prohibited the use of any permanent materials, such as concrete, stone, and brick; as a result, the vast majority of houses are built from mud, wattle and daub, wood, and sheet iron, lower-quality materials that are more vulnerable to erosion and damage. Structures built from more permanent materials are torn down and dismantled. The legal control of the architecture of Kibera enforces the characteristics of a slum and the visual markers of urban poverty. Furthermore, the building codes and "unauthorized" designation of the community also altered the relationships of Kibera's inhabitants to the state, and later to the UN and NGOs. Residents became slum dwellers rather than homeowners; through legislation and building codes, they were now rendered humanitarian subjects. Although the landlords and city provide no infrastructure to unauthorized settlements, the government also prohibits its residents from installing their own. This infrastructural double-bind results in some creative if unpleasant solutions: numerous garden hoses running underfoot through red mud carry residential water supply lines; plastic bottles full of water puncture the corrugated metal roofs to serve as skylights in the absence of electricity; the lack of sanitary waste lines results in "flying toilets," bags of human waste flung over rooftops as far as possible from their point of origin.

Despite the government's policies against permanent settlement, people continued to live in Kibera after it was declared unauthorized, and new arrivals from rural villages who were seeking jobs in postindependence Nairobi settled there by the thousands. With the influx of new arrivals, non-Nubians became the majority, with Kikuyu, Luo, and Luhya from Western Kenya forming the largest groups. By the early 1970s landlords were renting out their properties in Kibera to significantly greater numbers of tenants than were initially housed in the slum, and because the government had largely withdrawn from the administration of Kibera, unchecked subdivisions were allowed to proliferate, creating an incredible density of unrecognized residents.

Why was Kibera declared unauthorized but also permitted to continue to exist? Certainly, the designation of a slum relieves the government of the responsibility to provide even basic services, and allows it to act on Kibera in ways that might otherwise be politically difficult, such as demolishing buildings when the state deems it necessary with no legal recourse for the residents. The precarious and undocumented land tenure system in Kibera allows landlords, many of whom are government officials, to benefit directly from the slum while providing little in the way of security or legal protection to the slum dwellers, who have no legal claim to the land. Targeted demolition of buildings in Nairobi's slums has historically been used by the government as a means of punishing political dissent or rewarding loyalty, both in the colonial and postindependence eras.

The precarity of land tenure in Kibera is evident along the route of the Kenya-Uganda Railway, which cuts through the slum. The railway, which once served as an unofficial boundary of Kibera but has since been absorbed as its area grew, is administered by the national government's Kenya Railways Corporation and provides a main channel for foot traffic through the dense neighborhoods. By some accounts, the railroad tracks are the only reliable route through the community, and it has been documented that a large number of public services and businesses are located along its tracks.[5] The railway serves also as a pathway to nearby areas adjacent to Kibera, where many residents are employed. The official 60-meter buffer zone prohibiting access to the railway has not slowed circulation along its course, nor has it stalled construction within this zone, despite occasional attempts by the Kenya Railways Corporation to clear the area. Eviction notices posted in the designated buffer zone through Kibera in 2004 were estimated to affect between 51,000 and 108,000 residents and business owners, a high number due, in part, to the many schools, hospitals, and churches that exist within the buffer zone of the railway tracks. Yet, at the same time, the Kenya Railways Corporation has leased out plots of land within 10 meters of the railway line, collecting rent on the same land which they periodically clear by force.[6]

5 See *Map Kibera Project*, goo.gl/dzOEnn.

6 Centre on Housing Rights and Evictions, *Listening to the Poor: Housing Rights in Nairobi, Kenya* (Geneva: Centre on Housing Rights and Evictions, 2005), 58.

So while it may seem like the quintessential "informal economy," Kibera is also eminently profitable to those who operate squarely within the bounds of the formal economic, political, and legal systems. Although its mud shacks might not look like desirable real estate investments, most are owned not by their residents, but by middle- and upper-class landlords living outside Kibera.[7] The majority of landlords are government officials and politicians, or at least have connections to officials, or are wealthy enough to pay bribes to them.[8] Illegal payment is often demanded by so-called chiefs in the Provincial Administration for new construction or building upgrades in the community, with payment enforced under the threat of violence by groups of young men.[9]

7 Robert Neuwirth, *Shadow Cities: A Billion Squatters, a New Urban World* (London: Routledge, 2004).

8 University of Nairobi report, cited in United Nations Human Settlements Programme, *The Challenge of Slums* (see note 3).

9 Paul M. Syagga, Winnie V. Mitullah, and Sarah Karirah-Gitau, *Nairobi Slum Upgrading Initiatives: Nairobi Situation Analysis. Consultative Report to GOK/UNCHS* (Nairobi: Government of Kenya and UN-Habitat, 2001).

Kibera's illegal status makes buildings located within the area potentially more profitable assets for these landlords than otherwise comparable properties within the formal land tenure system, as they have no responsibility to provide or maintain basic services, such as electricity, latrines, water, and trash collection. Owning structures in Kibera is therefore a reliable investment, because it is one that costs almost nothing to maintain, and the steady supply of tenants ensures continued profits. It is estimated that more than 80 percent of residents are paying tenants of the buildings they occupy.[10]

10 Washington Olima and Sarah Karirah-Gitau, *Land Tenure and Tenancy Concerns and Issues in Kibera* (Final report, unpublished, WSP-ESA, The World Bank, KUESP Preparatory Task Group, 2000).

Humanitarian Government

The decades-long transition from a Nubian land reserve to an unauthorized settlement on public land has created rival claims to the ownership and control of Kibera, and a corresponding range of interests has complicated various attempts to improve or eliminate the slum. Today, the Kenyan government and the Nubian community both claim the right to the land, while the structures are owned by individual landlords and rented to the slum's inhabitants. More recently, a host of both local and international NGOs have come to operate within the slum, sometimes occupying plots of contested land through negotiations with the Kenyan government.

A facility in Kibera providing bathrooms and drinking water, built with funding from UN-Habitat

These nongovernmental organizations are also powerful actors in the politics of the slum. There are between 6,000 and 15,000 NGOs currently working in Kibera, ranging from community-based religious organizations to prominent international NGOs. Depending on which figures for Kibera's population you find credible, this number could represent as many as one NGO for every fifteen residents. The list of NGOs operating in Kibera includes Médecins Sans Frontières (MSF), World Vision, the African Medical and Research Foundation (AMREF), as well as UN agencies like UNICEF and UN-Habitat, and innumerable smaller NGOs, many of which are faith-based. This plethora of aid organizations provides services in Kibera that are elsewhere administered by the state, ranging from education to sanitation and using donations from individuals, governments, and corporations around the world. More than any other slum in Nairobi, Kibera exists as a confluence of different kinds of aid, governmental and nongovernmental, due in large part to its heavy media presence and prominence in international relief aid discourse.[11] Whether intentionally or not, the projects of these groups benefit indirectly from the notion that Kibera is an out-of-control slum, a mounting crisis that demands and justifies their interventions.

11 Caroline S. Archambault, Joost de Laat, and Eliya Msiyaphazi Zulu, "Urban Services and Child Migration to the Slums of Nairobi," *World Development* 40, no. 9 (2012): 1854–69.

Counting

Numbers play a major role in sustaining the superlatives that are part of Kibera's mythos. While it is frequently referred to in the press as "the largest slum in Africa," current population estimates range from under 200,000 to over 2,000,000. A 2001 UN publication estimated that there were 377,624 residents,[12] but by 2007 the UN stated that "the estimated total population in the settlement ranges from 600,000 to 1,000,000 inhabitants."[13] This leap in population estimates for the area occurred during an increase in the financial resources that UN-Habitat devoted to humanitarian work in the community, after the adoption of the Millennium Development Goals, which allowed for more detailed population data to be gathered. The shift in the numbers also coincides with the initiation of a slum upgrading program in Kibera, a joint project of the Government of Kenya and UN-Habitat. At the lower range of the estimates, according to the 2009 Kenyan census, there are a mere 170,070 residents,[14] and according to the independent Map Kibera Project, headed by geographer Stefano Marras, there are between 220,000 to 250,000 residents.[15]

12 Syagga, Mitullah, and Karirah-Gitau, *Nairobi Slum Upgrading Initiative*, UN HABITAT report (see note 9).

13 Sara Candiracci and Raakel Syrjänen, *UN HABITAT and the Kenya Slum Upgrading Program* (Nairobi: United Nations Settlement Program, 2007), 24.

14 Muchiri Karanja, "Myth Shattered: Kibera Numbers Fail to Add Up," *Daily Nation*, September 3, 2010, goo.gl/SoaQKy.

15 "Maps and Statistics," *Map Kibera Project*, accessed March 9, 2017, goo.gl/zaNhjN.

Comparing these conflicting visions of the city, the range of techniques for making Kibera legible to different interests becomes apparent. Population counts have been conducted using a variety of methods and techniques, from the door-to-door surveys of the Map Kibera Project to the remote sensing imagery and aerial photography of the UN estimates. Kibera's epithet, the "largest slum in Africa," is thus less an absolute truth than a product of the techniques employed to make the slum visible. Maintaining the image of "Africa's largest slum" is important in justifying the UN's slum upgrading program in Kibera, and by extension other development projects throughout Africa under the framework of the Millennium Development Goals. The rendering of a humanitarian crisis and the insistence on a pressing need for relief and development aid, rather than land tenure or political reform, is a means of bringing a contested space and population under the authority of international institutions. It is the process by which humanitarian space, and humanitarian subjects, are produced. Through a combination of compelling statistics and a series of government policies from the colonial era to the present, residents have been transformed into an innumerable mass of slum dwellers that therefore requires techniques of enumeration in order to be reincorporated into the formal economy and land tenure systems. This is the paradox of Kibera, a place where unrecognized residents are forbidden from improving their situation, but are then pressed into the narrative of an intractable urban crisis and subsequently relocated with the help of international NGOs in a locally protested but internationally acclaimed "participatory" process of slum upgrading.

The Kibera Soweto East Resource Center, a community-based organization that offers health care and youth programs

KENSUP

Currently the UN's dominant model of urban development in slum areas, the Participatory Slum Upgrading Programme (PSUP) projects involve community groups in the proposed interventions in their neighborhoods. The focus on participation aims to build broad support for measures undertaken by the UN in cooperation with municipal and national governments, local civil society groups, and funders in international financial institutions like the World Bank. The PSUP framework is intended to place the people whose neighborhood is being transformed at the forefront of the decision-making process.

The PSUP model was launched by UN-Habitat in 2008, and reflects a shift, at least in nomenclature, from the earlier model of SUPs—slum upgrading, but without the participation. The expansive, ongoing reconstruction process in Kibera—the Kenya Slum Upgrading Program (KENSUP), a pilot project which has built dozens of multistory towers on sites inside and adjacent to the slum—is from this earlier model of slum upgrading, and the limitations of its methodologies might account for the UN's new emphasis on participation.

KENSUP was initiated in 2000 and formalized during the observance of World Habitat Day on October 4, 2004, in a joint declaration by the executive director of UN-Habitat and the Kenyan Ministry of Housing. The program's intention was to provide 45,000 units of housing annually, starting with a pilot project in the Soweto East neighborhood of Kibera. KENSUP is administered by the Ministry of Housing and jointly funded by the government of Kenya and the UN-HABITAT/World Bank Cities Alliance. KENSUP is intended to align with the UN's Millennium Development Goals (MDGs), which have since been renamed the Sustainable Development Goals (SDGs). As described in a UN-Habitat document issued in 2008, "UN-Habitat's KENSUP strategy draws its main concepts and principles from the Habitat Agenda, which guides the agency's activities; the Millennium Development Goals (MDGs); the government of Kenya's KENSUP Strategy; and the principles from the Water for African Cities II Programme."[16] The purpose of forming KENSUP, says Tirop Kosgey, permanent secretary of the Kenyan Ministry of Housing, was to fast-track the achievement of the MDGs and improve access to basic services by the year 2020.[17] The UN's role in the project is carried out from UN-Habitat's Nairobi offices. It is touted as a success by the UN, and even highlighted for publicity and fund-raising purposes.

16 Raakel Syrjänen et al., *UN-Habitat and the Kenya Slum Upgrading Programme: Strategy Document* (Nairobi: United Nations Human Settlements Programme, 2008), 27, goo.gl/JWMs25.

17 Walter Menya, "Kenya: Joint Efforts Bring Hope to Thousands of Slum Dwellers," *Daily Nation*, March 28, 2008.

The KENSUP housing in Kibera under construction. The road was cleared and paved to facilitate the movement of materials and equipment to the building site.

Through KENSUP, UN-Habitat has targeted Kibera as a proving ground for its slum upgrading program. It has been presented as a test run and an opportunity to refine a process that could be replicated around the world. KENSUP is also intended to be generalized more locally to other neighborhoods in Nairobi. In announcing the partnership with UN-Habitat to form KENSUP, Mwai Kibaki, president of Kenya, said the program would improve access to shelter, water and sanitation, education, health, security, and employment to an estimated population of almost six million who live in the unauthorized neighborhoods around the city.[18]

18 "Statement by the HE President of the Republic of Kenya and Commander-in-Chief of the Armed Force Hon. Mwai Kibaki, During the Special Session of the African Ministerial Conference on Housing and Development (AMCHUD) on 3rd April 2006 at Gigiri, Nairobi, goo.gl/EICT03.

But while it is intended to be an exemplary model, KENSUP is also somewhat of an outlier among recent urban planning approaches to slum improvements in that it is one of the few slum upgrading processes worldwide that has led to the large-scale relocation of residents outside the slum. Many recent and contemporary slum upgrading programs focus on in situ development efforts through the provision of infrastructural components and "incremental housing" strategies, an updated version of the "sites and services" model first pioneered in the 1970s. Dandora, located in eastern Nairobi, was the first sites and services project implemented by the World Bank in the mid-1970s.[19] Unlike the KENSUP pilot program, these projects work through small interventions in the existing slum, rather than large-scale demolition and relocation of the slum's inhabitants.

19 Patrick Wakely and Elizabeth Riley, "The Case for Incremental Housing," *Cities Alliance Policy Research and Working Papers Series* 1 (June 2011), 11, goo.gl/O8Su46.

The dislocation of Kibera's residents through the slum upgrading process stems in part from the program's continuities with Kenyan government policies from the 1960s and 1970s that promoted the demolition of unauthorized neighborhoods coupled with construction of public housing. These policies were enacted to address a large-scale rural-to-urban migration following independence, in response to the increased mobility and civil rights that were now extended to the African population of Kenya. Despite the lifting of restrictions on residency and movement and the extending of the city's boundaries, the patterns of economic and racial segregation of the colonial era continued after independence.

Looking over the rooftops of Kibera, to the new housing being built by the Kenya Slum Upgrading Program

The geography of segregation was reasserted, albeit indirectly, by government policies that were intended to address the rapid growth of the city. The Nairobi Metropolitan Growth Strategy, introduced in 1973, intended to develop "integrated self-contained metropolitan neighborhoods," but instead reinforced Nairobi's "island urbanism," producing a series of physically and socially disconnected, inward-facing enclaves of single-story slums and multistory social housing built by the government.[20]

20 Omenya, "Island Urbanism: Spatial Segregation in Nairobi" (see note 1).

These earlier programs were financed by the Kenyan government's National Housing Corporation, which created high-rise redevelopments inside or adjacent to preexisting slum areas, in a style similar to what KENSUP would later propose. While some of these proposals successfully reached their target populations, a previous attempt to "upgrade" Kibera, the Nyayo Highrise Estate, missed the mark when cost overruns resulted in mortgages too high for its intended beneficiaries to repay. The original occupants sold their units to middle-income households, presumably to return to Kibera. The KENSUP program learned from this mistake and designed the new housing for Kibera to lower standards than Nyayo Highrise in an effort to make the units less desirable to the middle class. However, their suitability to the populations for which they are intended remains questionable as there are numerous reports of families relocated from Soweto East to the new housing who choose to sublet their assigned housing units, either partially or entirely, and even relocate completely back into Kibera.[21]

21 Bob Hendricks, "Housing and the Urban Poor in Kenya: Opportunities for Increased Partnerships and Innovative Practices," in *Affordable Housing in the Urban Global South: Seeking Sustainable Solutions*, ed. Jan Bredenoord, Paul Van Lindert, and Peer Smets (Abingdon: Routledge, 2014), 368. Also reported in Gregory Scruggs, "Turning Kibera's Mud Huts into Apartment Towers," *Citiscope*, August 7, 2015, goo.gl/X7DxVb; and Lukorito W. Jones, "Kibera Upgrading Project Full of Contradictions," *Daily Nation*, June 25, 2015, goo.gl/h8Ms5g, among others.

The first group of residential towers was constructed on the outskirts of the slum, southeast of the Soweto East neighborhood. This cluster of buildings is known as the Decanting Site because it is intended to serve as temporary housing for residents who were displaced when the KENSUP program cleared the land on which the permanent housing would be built. The standard units in the buildings at the Decanting Site are 50 m^2 and have three rooms, compared with the 80 m^2 that is typical for middle-income housing in Kenya.[22] The towers are comprised of vertically stacked apartments, each unit designed to accommodate a separate family. However, in Kibera, a family may consist of three generations and cousins, who would typically live in close proximity. Relocation means either separating the extended family into multiple housing units at high cost, or being confined all together in a space smaller than what they could afford to share in Kibera. Video footage from the move-in day at the Decanting Site, recorded by journalists from Voice of Kibera, captures the residents' reactions to the conditions of the housing units. Some are surprised and welcome the change; others are dismayed at the distance from their former homes, the cost of rent, and the unreliable electricity; and some declare that they will immediately move back to their homes in Kibera, which are both more convenient and more affordable.[23]

22 Alfred Omenya and Marie Huchzermeyer, "Slum Upgrading in the Complex Context of Policy Change: The Case of Nairobi," in *Informal Settlements: A Perpetual Challenge?*, ed. Marie Huchzermeyer and Aly Karam (Cape Town: University of Cape Town Press, 2007), 298.

23 Goo.gl/yKQckN

The KENSUP Decanting Site

While the KENSUP housing provides more reliable water, electricity, and sanitary services than was available to residents in the slum, the infrastructural services are not as dependable as many had hoped. In a series of 2015 interviews with the *Daily Nation*, the highest selling daily newspaper in Kenya, residents of the Decanting Site complained that the infrastructure in the new housing units was insufficient, saying, "Many problems that we hoped to escape from in the slum have followed us" and "We experience acute water shortages here. For instance, blocks A, B, C, P, and H have not had running water for more than a month now. Most residents have to queue for a long time for water."[24] These complaints are a serious challenge to the successes of the KENSUP program thus far, though the response of the director of KENSUP, Charles Sikuku, may provide insight into the urban planning and policy strategies that have led to the current situation. Sikuku stated that, "According to the Sectional Properties Act, the residents themselves are required to form management committees to run the place. If any problems arise, it is their responsibility to resolve them through the committees."[25] The approach he describes is in some ways strikingly similar to the conditions in the slum—residents pay rent to the government or its employees and are responsible for the provision of their own infrastructural services. The key difference is that in the KENSUP system, after approximately twenty-five years of paying rent, residents will become owners of their housing units with formally recognized land tenure.

24 Jones, "Kibera Upgrading Project Full of Contradictions" (see note 21).

25 Ibid.

While the payoff after the twenty-five-year rent-to-own period is significant, many residents in the new housing struggle to pay more per month to rent KENSUP's apartments than they did in Kibera. The new units in the KENSUP buildings cost twenty-six to thirty-three dollars per month to rent, which may not sound like much, but accounts for more than half of an average resident's monthly income. Purchasing a unit would require an income of at least that for fifteen to twenty years,[26] likely longer due to the competing costs of food, sanitation, water, and other necessities. Most Kibera residents have irregular income and pay monthly rents of around seven dollars, a situation that makes the housing provided by KENSUP an unrealistic solution for the poor of Nairobi's slums without simultaneously dramatically changing the economic life of the city.

26 Omenya and Huchzermeyer, "Slum Upgrading in the Complex Context of Policy Change," 299 (see note 22).

But perhaps more deleterious than increased rent is the potential loss of income for the residents as a consequence of their separation from the economic life of Kibera. Many residents stand

The KENSUP Decanting Site, a group of multistory buildings on the edge of Kibera that provide temporary housing to residents displaced by the demolition required to clear land in Kibera for the construction of permanent housing

to lose the ability to run the tax-free small businesses that they operated informally in the slum. A small shop that would have been operated in the front room of a single-story house in Kibera cannot be accommodated by the vertical organization of the residential towers in the KENSUP blocks, as the lack of foot traffic in front of individual housing units precludes the possibility of a profitable home business, particularly for women who are simultaneously providing childcare within the home. The architectural form of KENSUP, the solution devised by the Kenyan government and its NGO partners to address the challenges of slum dwellers, has eliminated the possibility of small-scale home businesses that existed in the single-story sprawl of Kibera rather than providing economic opportunities for advancement and security.

As an alternative to the markets of Kibera, women who live in the KENSUP estates set up small stands in the yard between the towers, selling fruits, vegetables, and small goods. But the market for such goods is small as the vendors are cut off from the larger catchment of customers by a wall around the perimeter of the site that separates the KENSUP project from Kibera. Nonresidents are technically not allowed to enter the KENSUP Decanting Site, though the guard posts are often left empty and passage into the walled compound is inconvenient but not particularly difficult. The policy is intended to discourage Kibera's squatters from moving into the new buildings without authorization, or building single-story shelters between the towers, but it also divides small business owners in KENSUP from their customer base in Kibera. The wall surrounding the site also limits the space allotted for the sellers, who are not permitted to set up stands on the other side. The majority of the women setting up markets and shops within the Decanting Site are financially responsible for their families and are disproportionately affected by the government's urban policies in a society which already manifests strong gender discrimination.[27] The burden of women's domestic role in Nairobi is further strained in the KENSUP housing, where informal childcare networks are disrupted and community support is not readily available. Their removal from their potential market base in the slum adds to these challenges a great economic burden for the women living in the Decanting Site.

27 United Nations Human Settlements Programme, *State of the World's Cities 2010/2011: Bridging the Urban Divide* (London: Earthscan, 2010), 43.

Participation

While the UN touts the participatory aspect of the process, the publicly available documentation of the KENSUP projects does not specify who was consulted or by what means they were chosen as the representatives of the community.[28] At the outset of the KENSUP project, a Settlement Executive Committee (SEC) was created as an elected council of representatives comprised of residents of Kibera. These individuals were designated as the points of contact and conduits of communication between the slum community and representatives of the governmental and NGO partners facilitating the KENSUP project.

28 United Nations Human Settlements Programme, *UN-HABITAT and the Kenya Slum Upgrading Programme: Strategy Document* (Nairobi: UN-Habitat, 2008).

We met a member of the SEC, James Mokoa, in a small room built into a shipping container near the entrance to Kibera that is the office of the SEC. The office sits at the rear of an enclosed yard off the main avenue into Kibera, Mbagathi Road, opposite another stack of shipping containers that houses UN-Habitat's site office. The yard and the offices were built as part of the construction of the main road into Kibera. Mbagathi Road, a paved thoroughfare leading from the highway, was built with funding from UN-Habitat during the initial phases of the KENSUP process, as were the small, fresh-looking shops that line its concrete sidewalk. To build the road required the demolition of hundreds of homes in Kibera's Soweto East neighborhood, but the road was also necessary for transporting the equipment and materials needed for the new KENSUP housing, to which it leads.

The local office of UN-Habitat in Kibera, on Mbagathi Road near the entrance to Kibera.

When we met in the SEC's offices, Mokoa acknowledged that although the UN had asked for regular SEC elections every few years, as of the time of our conversation in 2013, there had not been a subsequent election after the first in 2004, and the majority of members of the SEC were no longer participating in the process or attending meetings with the UN representatives. He also mentioned that the latest residency records on which the UN was basing its housing plan were from 2004, which were current at the initiation of KENSUP but were well out-of-date by 2013, and in his view could not possibly be used to allocate housing to particular families who had not been counted in the 2004 registry but were nevertheless displaced by the demolition of their neighborhood.

The attempt at forming a representative community council notwithstanding, participation in the PSUP process in Kibera has been exclusionary from the beginning. Although the UN helped create the SEC, the Nubians, Kibera's original residents, claim to never have been consulted. Not surprisingly, they have voiced the strongest opposition to the project, and Nubian leaders are organizing their community to refuse the government relocation effort unless they are compensated for their homes. Yusuf Diab, secretary of the Nubian Council of Elders, argued against the KENSUP plan, saying that it would "make us tenants of the government for the rest of our lives."[29] The Nubians are considered a stateless population by the UNHCR, and are largely excluded from Kenyan political life. The status of their land rights in Kibera remains unresolved: originally granted 1,600 hectares by the British, their current official landholdings in Kibera have been reduced, since independence, to 115 hectares with the remaining land in dispute.[30] Ibrahim Diaby, a Nubian elder, stated that, in his opinion, improvements should be made to the existing housing in the slum instead of relocating the population. "My house has water and electricity, but I'm restricted from putting up a permanent building because the government says the land belongs to them. It's a question of natural justice. We've lived in Kibera long before Nairobi was Nairobi, long before Kenya was Kenya."[31]

29 Susan Anyangu, "Kenya: Foreigners in Their Homeland," Inter Press Service, November 14, 2009, goo.gl/PO6xvr.

30 Centre on Housing Rights and Evictions, *Listening to the Poor* (see note 6).

31 "Kenya Begins Huge Slum Clearance," BBC News, last updated September 16, 2009, goo.gl/UNkleM.

The bulldozing of thousands of homes is justified by Kibera's designation as a slum, and is abetted by the rhetoric of community participation. KENSUP appears to flout international housing rights law, which requires that social housing strategies "should reflect extensive genuine consultation with, and participation by, all of those affected, including the homeless, the inadequately housed and their representatives."[32] Interviewed by the international housing rights organization COHRE at the site of the housing development, a UN-Habitat official dismissed human rights organizations giving voice to community concerns as interfering with the process of the SUP.[33]

32 UN Committee on Economic, Social and Cultural Rights (CESCR), *General Comment No. 4: The Right to Adequate Housing (Art.11 (1) of the Covenant)*, December 13, 1991, E/1992/23, goo.gl/CvQLR7.

33 Omenya and Huchzermeyer, "Slum Upgrading in the Complex Context of Policy Change," 305 (see note 22).

Leaving aside its seeming indifference to a participatory process, the KENSUP program has fallen short of its objective of fast-tracking the Millennium Development Goals. KENSUP, like previous Kenyan policies of slum clearance, has not kept pace with the rate of displacement caused by demolitions. To date only 600 units have been created to house roughly 1,800 people, while at the outset of the project, the village of Soweto East, the area whose residents the new housing was intended to accommodate, housed 60,000 people.[34] At this rate, rehousing the population that the KENSUP program is intended to benefit would take centuries. The delays in the construction are in part due to the resistance of landlords to the slum upgrading program, since the process of constructing new housing requires cataloguing the existing structures and their residents, which potentially exposes the landlords to questions about their lawful status as owners and eventually implies the demolition of existing structures on the site of the new construction, which comes at a cost to the landlords, many of whom are government employees and politicians. The process of slum upgrading has therefore proceeded very slowly and with limited effect.

34 Laura MacPherson, "Participatory Approaches to Slum Upgrading and Poverty Reduction in African Cities," *Hydra: Interdisciplinary Journal of Social Sciences* 1, no. 1 (2013): 89.

For better or worse, the landlords aren't the only parties with a financial interest in the slum upgrading project. In fact the Kenyan Housing Authority, which administers the KENSUP project, is financed by a bond issued by the US-based private sector company Overseas Private Investment Corporation (OPIC).[35] However, it is unlikely that the costs for the KENSUP project could ever be repaid with the rents paid by Kibera's residents, as the funding mechanism for the new housing stock is appropriate only for middle-income households. The financing structure behind the housing project therefore gives credibility to fears that KENSUP is not a self-evidently altruistic gesture, but a concerted effort to displace the residents of Kibera and construct profitable, middle-income, high-rise developments on the site of the former ethnic reserve.

35 Omenya and Huchzermeyer, "Slum Upgrading in the Complex Context of Policy Change," 304 (see note 22).

EPZs and Humanitarian Industry

Not all of Nairobi's slums have as long a history as Kibera. Some, like Mukuru in eastern Nairobi, are relatively new and have existed only for a few decades. Mukuru dates to the mid-1970s, when factory workers in the newly created Industrial Zone began to build shacks near to their workplaces. With the growth of industrial processing, Mukuru grew as well, and now houses around 600,000 people in the disused area along the Ngong River, between the Industrial Zone and Mombasa Road, the highway that leads to the airport.

The neighborhood of Mukuru known as Commercial Village was one of the first settlement areas to be built up near the Industrial Zone, starting in 1973. According to surveys of the slum, 65 percent of its roughly 6,000 residents work in the nearby factories and 99 percent are tenants.[36] Unlike the residents of other slums in Nairobi, Mukuru's residents were not originally landless or displaced from other areas, but rather resettled voluntarily in order to have access to jobs and save on transportation costs. In that sense, Mukuru, like Kibera, can hardly be considered informal, as it is so closely tied to the development strategies pursued by the municipal and national governments.

36 Pamoja Trust, *Nairobi Inventory* (n.p., 2009), 48–49.

In the early 1990s the national government sought to accelerate industrial development in the country. To that end, the Sameer Industrial Park was created in 1991, the first of several export processing zones (EPZs) throughout the country. Sameer Industrial Park consists of 20 factory buildings of around 1,500 square meters each, spread out across 10 hectares of land. Eight of the buildings are legally part of the EPZ and enjoy a range of advantages that include abatements from corporate taxes and customs. Sameer also provides warehouses for Médecins Sans Frontières, one of several relief organizations that use the Industrial Zone's facilities as a logistical hub. Perhaps ironically, these relief organizations operate in an industrial complex that benefits from the labor provided by the same slums in which these or similar organizations provide aid and services.

Walking along Enterprise Road, the main route leading from Mombasa Road through the EPZ area, we noticed narrow, dusty alleys branching off and leading into pockets of the Mukuru slums. Continuing on the main road, we passed Indu Fresh EPZ Ltd., Solitaire Gems EPZ Ltd., and KenCall EPZ Ltd., tax-free operations within the Sameer EPZ that deal in agricultural exports, diamonds, and call center services. More germane to our interests is Techno Relief Services EPZ, Ltd., another company housed in a warehouse in the Sameer EPZ.

The Techno Relief Group describes itself as "global suppliers of humanitarian aid and relief goods, providing end-to-end global logistical support to NGOs and aid agencies with offices ranging from worldwide warehouses and a team dedicated to emergency relief, development, and capacity building."[37] Since its founding in Kenya in 1987 as Techno Relief Services, the company has expanded from a local operation established to coordinate logistics and supplies for humanitarian operations in Kenya to a global manufacturer of relief products, beginning with the TechnoTarp, which they first brought to market to meet the need for durable tarp materials following the crisis in Sudan. Techno Group has since expanded its production and distribution operations around the world, setting up successive regional offices in Mumbai, India (2004), Kampala, Uganda (2004), Juba, South Sudan (2006), Khartoum, North Sudan (2007), Delaware, United States (2010), Hatay, Turkey (2013), and Goma, Democratic Republic of Congo (2014). They have also recently opened an office in the Netherlands to represent the company's interests in Europe.

37 Home page, *Techno Relief Group*, goo.gl/gatXlt.

Initially only a logistical support company, Techno Group has expanded and diversified its manufacturing and services to include water technologies and well engineering, educational materials for UNICEF, camp kitchens and sanitary facilities for IDP camps, and hygienic and first-aid kits. In 2014 they added pharmaceuticals under the new division Techno Pharma. Their clients include international organizations such as UNDP, UNHCR, WFP, and UNICEF, as well as all of the major international NGOs: the International Committee of the Red Cross (ICRC), Concern Worldwide, Care International, Oxfam International, Catholic Relief Services, Caritas, the Salvation Army, World Vision, and Médecins Sans Frontières.

Techno Group is not the only relief-aid logistics company that operates out of Nairobi's free zones. Near the Sameer EPZ, the Sandton Park/Sunflag EPZ leases space to other relief supply companies, including Spartan Relief EPZ, Ltd., based in Kenya, and Noor Relief Services EPZ, Ltd., a humanitarian products company headquartered in Karachi. The extraterritoriality of humanitarian operations, which in the name of humanity and justified by the latest state of emergency regularly glide across the jurisdictions of national governments, joins here with the extraterritoriality of global capital in the production and distribution of goods in a smooth and seamless duty-free zone that creates an economic coherence at a transnational scale.

Footpaths cutting across the grounds of the meteorological station in the Industrial Zone, made by workers walking to the factories from the nearby settlements.

In between the long-span sheds of the EPZs near Enterprise Road is a large, enclosed, grassy field. Before visiting the site in person, we had seen the area on satellite images, noting that it was owned by the Kenyan Meteorological Department, and houses a transmission station. The field is enclosed on all sides by a tall fence, presumably to keep the operations and workers of the factories from spilling over into the meteorological station. Standing on the field, one observes what satellites miss: that the apparent solidity of boundaries drawn as lines on a plan leaves open another dimension of activity: holes where the fence had been cut and peeled up, leading to paths across the field that were worn from workers walking to and from their places of employment and their homes in the surrounding settlements and estates. These lines of movement slip through the demarcations and boundaries, cutting new sectional short circuits between segregated areas and marking new paths and connections between sites kept separate by walls and fences. In its planning and design, the meteorological facility, like the Industrial Zone, had not anticipated the need to account for or accommodate the excess that the zone produces: the lives and movements of the human labor that the zone requires to produce the effect of seamlessness. The slums suggest the hidden friction of the zone's smooth space, and the holes in the fence point to the limits of architecture to effect total control over the bodies of the subjects it incorporates.

The clustering of Techno Group and the other humanitarian relief enterprises in the Industrial Zone is likely not accidental, as their neighbor on Enterprise Road is the ICRC Logistics Center, and the ICRC's main warehouse facility for Kenya is directly across Mombasa Road. The Logistics Center building is a notably unglamorous concrete block warehouse with an anonymous facade, enclosed by a concrete block wall with razor wire. Were it not for the ICRC flag waving from the roof, it could easily be mistaken for any other warehouse in the zone. This is the other architecture of the humanitarian organizations whose better known and better appointed buildings are located across town in the wealthy northwest suburbs of Nairobi. The centerpiece of that more recognized humanitarian district, known as the Blue Zone, is the UN complex located in the suburb of Gigiri.

The ICRC's Logistics Center, located in the Industrial Zone

UNON

In 1974 the Kenyan government granted land to the UN to construct the organization's Africa headquarters. The UN had been evaluating different African cities for the potential site of their headquarters, ultimately selecting Nairobi for its relative stability, which allowed it to serve as a neutral platform from which to manage operations in surrounding nations experiencing conflicts and disasters. For the new complex, now officially named the UN Office at Nairobi (UNON), Kenya gifted the UN 56 hectares of land in the Gigiri neighborhood, located in the well-to-do northwestern suburbs of the city.

The first phase of construction at UNON was completed in 1975, designed by the Kenyan architect David Mutiso. Mutiso is a prominent figure in Kenyan postindependence architecture, known for being the first non-European member of the Architectural Association of Kenya and the head of the Ministry of Public Works from 1967 to 1974, a period when many of the important public institutional buildings were under construction in the city. Mutiso also was one of the designers of the Kenyatta International Conference Center, opened in 1974 in Nairobi's central business district, which remained the tallest tower in Nairobi until the mid-2000s. His firm Mutiso Menezes International continues today to operate out of an office in Parklands, Nairobi.

In 1976 the first UN agency to be located in what is now UNON moved into the Gigiri compound. UNEP had been headquartered in Nairobi since 1972, the first major UN agency to have its headquarters in Africa. Since then, Nairobi has become the diplomatic hub of Africa, thanks largely to UNON. The complex's facilities and land area were expanded over the years, most recently with a new energy-neutral building housing the world headquarters of UN-Habitat and UNEP. The building, which opened in March 2011 and was designed by Nairobi architects Beglin Woods, provides 16,500 square meters of office space, mostly to the two main agencies. The complex now comprises 38 buildings spread out over 140 hectares and is home to 24 agencies and about 3,000 staff members, about 30 percent of whom are foreign residents.[38]

38 See United Nations Environment Programme, *Building for the Future: A United Nations Showcase in Nairobi* (Nairobi: UNEP Division of Communifcations and Public Information, 2011).

The interior courtyard of the UN-Habitat offices at UNON

UNON, like the other UN regional offices and headquarters in New York City, enjoys the benefits of extraterritorial status. Legally, the land on which UNON is built is an international zone, governed by international law and administered by the UN. Consistent with its status as a spatiojuridical loophole, the UNON campus has adopted the appearance of a park, a hybrid between an office park and a nature preserve, touted by the UN as a "green lung" for the city. The extensive parkland included in the complex is said by the UNEP to be home to 600 indigenous tree species, native birds, monkeys, and other small animals, all of which can be observed by visiting the agency's Gigiri Nature Trail, a path through the park that is intended to simultaneously make use of some of the 27 hectares that were deemed unbuildable and showcase the agency's commitment to the local environment.

Across the road from the UNON complex is the US embassy in Nairobi. The embassy opened in 2003, replacing the earlier embassy in central Nairobi, which was destroyed in 1998 by a bomb attack in which more than two hundred people, mostly Kenyans in an adjacent tower, were killed, and for which Al Qaeda claimed responsibility. After the bombing, the embassy was relocated from the city center to Gigiri, benefitting from the area's greater security. A memorial to the victims of the 1998 bombing now stands in the UNON gardens across the road.

The UNON complex and the US embassy are located within a larger area of the city officially designated by the UN as the Blue Zone. The Blue Zone was mapped out by the UN in the aftermath of the 2003 bombing of the UN's headquarters at the Canal Hotel in Baghdad and the 1998 bombing of the US embassies in Nairobi and Dar es Salaam, Tanzania. Located in the northwest suburbs of Nairobi, and centered on the Gigiri UN Complex, the Blue Zone is approved by the UN as a secure sector of the city for international staff of the UN and associated NGOs and aid organizations. The Blue Zone also includes the embassies of Brazil, Canada, Ecuador, Eritrea, Estonia, Finland, Madagascar, Malawi, Malaysia, Morocco, the Netherlands, and Pakistan. The area's name riffs on the famous Green Zone, the district of Baghdad secured by the US military for the operations of the coalition forces and their allied organizations. In Nairobi, the Blue Zone is similarly a secured area for the free and safe movement of the international population of diplomats, aid workers, employees of multinational firms, and associated consultants.

The Assembly Hall at the UN Office at Nairobi (UNON)

The Blue Zone is characterized by the island urbanism described by Alfred Omenya: most foreigners take cabs or hire personal drivers to move between secured, gated compounds, from home, to the children's school, to the office, to the mall, to the restaurant, and back home. But overlaying this archipelago is another, as Nairobi's slums are often immediately adjacent to wealthy areas,

A path between two walls on the edge of Kibera. The wall on the left is the edge of Kibera; the wall on the right is the boundary of the Golf Course neighborhood.

often separated by a wall, sometimes covered in glass shards, making a hard break between dire poverty and the relative leisure of Nairobi's international class; Kibera directly abuts the Royal Nairobi Golf Club and the upper-middle-class suburban developments Golf Course Estate and Ngumo Estate, separated only by a high wall. In fact, one of the popular points of entry to Kibera for curious international tourists is to join one of the "slum tours" that leaves from a nearby mall. Similar to the relationship between Mukuru and the EPZs, networks that connect the islands of the wealthy suburbs and those that connect the slums are not entirely separate. They rely on a kind of topology in which the lines that connect them also fold into boundaries between them. The islands give way to a dense bundle of paths between them that simultaneously articulates their separation and their conjoining. On the southern edge of Kibera, the settlement is bounded by a new highway, the Southern Bypass Road, which separates the Decanting Site from the rest of Kibera, and separates Kibera from the middle-class suburb to its south, while connecting the Industrial Zone to the western suburbs of Nairobi, allowing motorists to bypass the city center. Most of the cost of the highway, about 85 percent of its total budget of $178 million USD, is being financed by China's EXIM Bank, and the design and construction is being handled by the China Road and Bridge Corporation.

The construction of the Southern Bypass Road, designed to connect Nairobi's wealthier neighborhoods while further cutting off Kibera from adjacent areas, suggests the limits to conceiving the city through the figure of island urbanism. While the spatial segregation of the city along racial and class lines certainly does produce a chain of insular, isolated neighborhoods connected to others across the city while isolated from their immediate context, the boundedness and localized space of the island is undone by the need to mobilize a host of international actors, from Chinese banks to free zone enterprises to the UN, working across multiple scales to sustain the illusion of the archipelago city. Perhaps one task for architecture is to imagine a different spatial figure, one that can account for the multiple interpenetrating scales of operations that characterize a city like Nairobi, scales that are not stably and hierarchically nested, with the local inside the national inside the international, but that are subject to all manner of reversals, comingling, and short circuits. Such a figure may be hard to imagine, simply because it defies the logic of scale that is so intuitively inherent in the idea of space. It may be that the space of a city like Nairobi requires a new way of conceiving of urban space, beyond the matryoshka doll of the local, national, and global.

The Southern Bypass Road, shown under construction, divides Kibera from the surrounding areas and the new housing at the Decanting Site.

TERRITORIES

Nairobi, Kenya

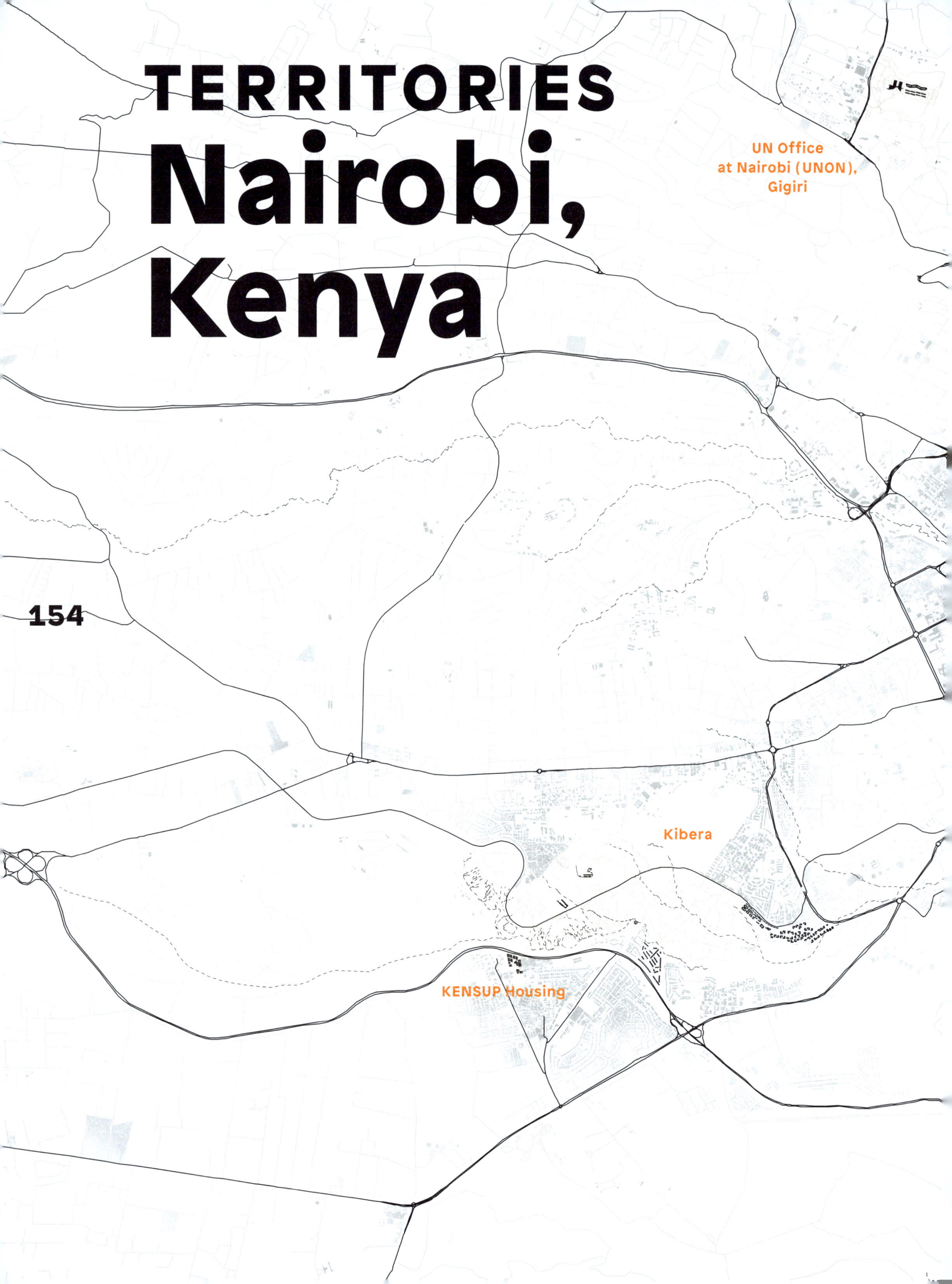

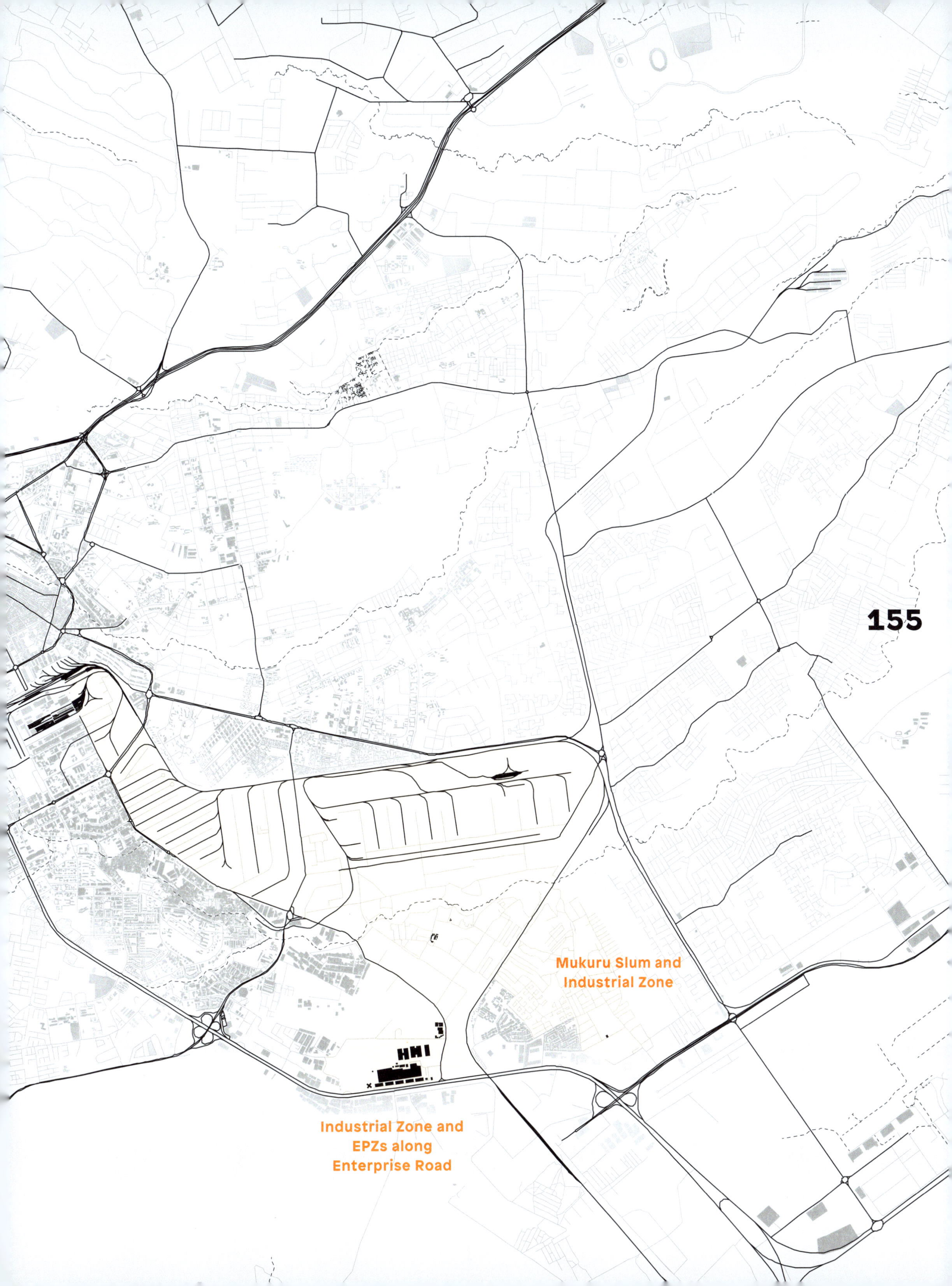
Mukuru Slum and
Industrial Zone
Industrial Zone and
EPZs along
Enterprise Road

Kibera

Kibera is possibly the largest slum in Nairobi with estimates ranging from 200,000 to more than 2,000,000 residents. It was first established in the late nineteenth century as an ethnic reserve for "detribalized" Nubians, originally from what is now Sudan, who had fought on behalf of the British in the King's African Rifles. After Kenyan independence, its population grew quickly, with members of other ethnic groups moving to the area to seek work in Nairobi. Today, it is the site of several projects to upgrade the slum, initiated by the UN, the Kenyan government, and international NGOs.

1

Matatu stop, entrance to Kibera

The matatu stop, at the entrance to Kibera on Mbagathi Way, is a major point of connection between the slum and other areas of the city. Matatus are privately owned minibuses that provide transportation to many Kenyans. Until the early 2000s, they were the only public transportation in Nairobi.

2002.02.04

2006.03.26

2016.10.23

2

Nyayo Highrise Estate

The Nyayo Highrise Estate was an earlier attempt to improve housing in Kibera, developed by the Kenyan government's National Housing Corporation. Finished in 1994, the project missed its target when the intended residents sold their units to middle-class buyers, most likely returning to their previous homes in Kibera.

2002.02.04

2016.10.23

3

Golf course

The Royal Nairobi Golf Club is directly adjacent to Kibera. It opened in 1906, catering to British living in Kenya, and is named after King George V of Britain. The upper-middle-class neighborhood surrounding it is known as Golf Course Estate due to its proximity.

2016.10.23

4

KENSUP (Kenya Slum Upgrading Programme) Decanting Site

The Decanting Site is a group of residential towers built by KENSUP to temporarily house residents of Kibera whose homes were destroyed to clear the site for new permanent housing. The project was intended to relieve overcrowding in the slum by moving residents off-site while the new housing was constructed.

2002.03.10

2007.01.21

2008.09.04

2016.10.23

5

NHC Langata Court

The complex of residential towers is another project by the National Housing Corporation attempting to improve conditions in Kibera by providing formalized housing.

2002.02.04

2007.01.21

2008.09.04

2016.10.23

6

MSF Kibera South Health Centre

Médecins Sans Frontières operates the Kibera South Health Centre, providing free clinic services to residents of the slum.

2011.01.16

2016.02.22

7

KENSUP Housing

KENSUP is a joint project of UN-Habitat and the Kenyan Ministry of Housing, an ambitious plan to add thousands of new units of housing in Kibera, starting with this pilot project in the village of Soweto East. Some thousands of residents were displaced to build the housing, which took from 2009 to 2014 to complete. The implementation of the plan has been difficult and slow from the beginning due to conflicts in the slum over the process and an alleged lack of consultation by the UN.

2009.07.27

2012.02.23

2013.01.18

2016.10.23

8

Kibera Primary School

The school was founded in 1953 by Nubian soldiers who had fought on behalf of the British. Later, the school was funded by the British, until being taken over by the Kenyan government after independence.

2016.10.23

9

Olympic Primary School

The school is partially funded by the British government, and ranks high on national achievement metrics. It was visited by British prime minister Gordon Brown in 2005.

2002.02.04

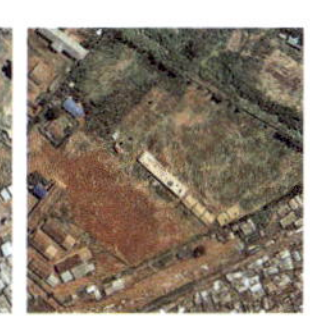
2009.07.27

2016.10.23

KENSUP Housing

The Kenya Slum Upgrading Programme is a joint project of the Kenyan Government and UN-Habitat to develop new multistory formal housing in Kibera. The project, which was initiated in 2000 and officially began operations in 2004, has been controversial, with concerns about the lack of community consultation, as well as delays in the schedule of the project.

1 KENSUP Decanting Site houses

The KENSUP Decanting Site is a complex of residential towers built to temporarily house residents displaced by the construction of new social housing in Kibera. The units are considered expensive by the standards of Kibera's residents, and most are too small to accommodate the extended family structures that are not uncommon in Kibera. The yard surrounding the housing is fenced off to prevent nonresidents from constructing self-built housing on the site.

2002.02.04

2007.01.21

2016.01.26

2016.10.23

2 Southern Bypass Road

The Southern Bypass Road defines part of the southern edge of Kibera and runs from the Industrial Zone to the western suburbs of Nairobi. The highway project was launched in 2012 and completed in 2016 with funding from the Chinese EXIM Bank. There is no exit for Kibera or the Decanting Site, but cars and matatus nonetheless pull off onto the shoulder at the overpass between Kibera and the Decanting Site to take passengers.

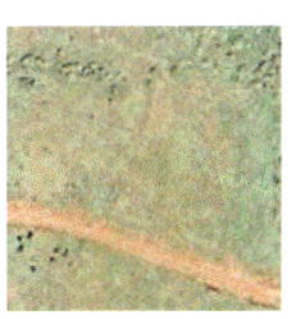
2004.12.23

2012.02.23

2016.10.23

3 Pedestrian path between Kibera and Decanting Site

The Decanting Site is accessible from Kibera through a passage under the Southern Bypass Road. The site is separated from Kibera by the Southern Bypass Road; consequently, while it provides its residents with a place to live, it is cut off from the economic and social networks of Kibera.

2002.02.04

2007.01.21

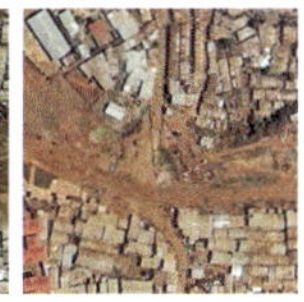
2012.02.23

2013.09.11

2016.10.23

Industrial Zone and EPZs along Enterprise Road

Nairobi's Industrial Zone began to be developed in the early 1970s. The area of the Industrial Zone along Enterprise Road is also the site of Kenya's first free trade zone, Sameer Industrial Park.

1 Sameer Industrial Park

Founded in 1993, the Sameer Industrial Park contains the first export processing zone (EPZ) established in Kenya. Of the twenty buildings that make up the complex, eight are part of the EPZ, including Techno Relief Services EPZ Ltd, a leading global supplier of relief-aid products.

2002.03.10

2008.06.29

2016.10.23

2 ICRC Logistics Center

The ICRC Logistics Center, the main warehouses for the relief organization's operations in Kenya, is located next door to the EPZ on Enterprise Road. A second complex of ICRC warehouses is nearby, across Mombasa Road.

2004.03.13

2016.10.23

3 Meteorological monitoring site

The Kenyan government operates a transmission station for meteorological data in an enclosed field near the EPZ. The fence surrounding the field is full of holes, where workers in the industrial zone have made new paths between their workplaces and their homes in the nearby slums and residential areas.

2004.03.13

2009.03.21

2016.10.23

Mukuru Slum and Industrial Zone

Situated southeast from the city center, the Industrial Zone was laid out as part of the 1948 Nairobi master plan. The growth of the zone in the last decades has also spurred the growth of new slums in the area, including the group of settlements known as Mukuru.

❶ Industrial Zone

The Industrial Zone began to be developed in the early 1970s, with areas for heavy and light industry, as well as oil and natural gas facilities.

2002.03.10

2016.10.23

❷ Hope Worldwide Kenya Mukuru

Hope Worldwide is a faith-based NGO offering health services in Mukuru.

2003.02.26

2016.10.23

❸ Mukuru Youth Initiative

Mukuru Youth Initiative is a youth-founded and -led community based organization in Mukuru.

2003.02.26

2016.10.23

❹ Ruben Centre

The Ruben Centre is a faith-based organization providing health, education, and financial services in the slum.

2007.01.21

2010.01.29

2016.10.23

UN Office at Nairobi (UNON), Gigiri

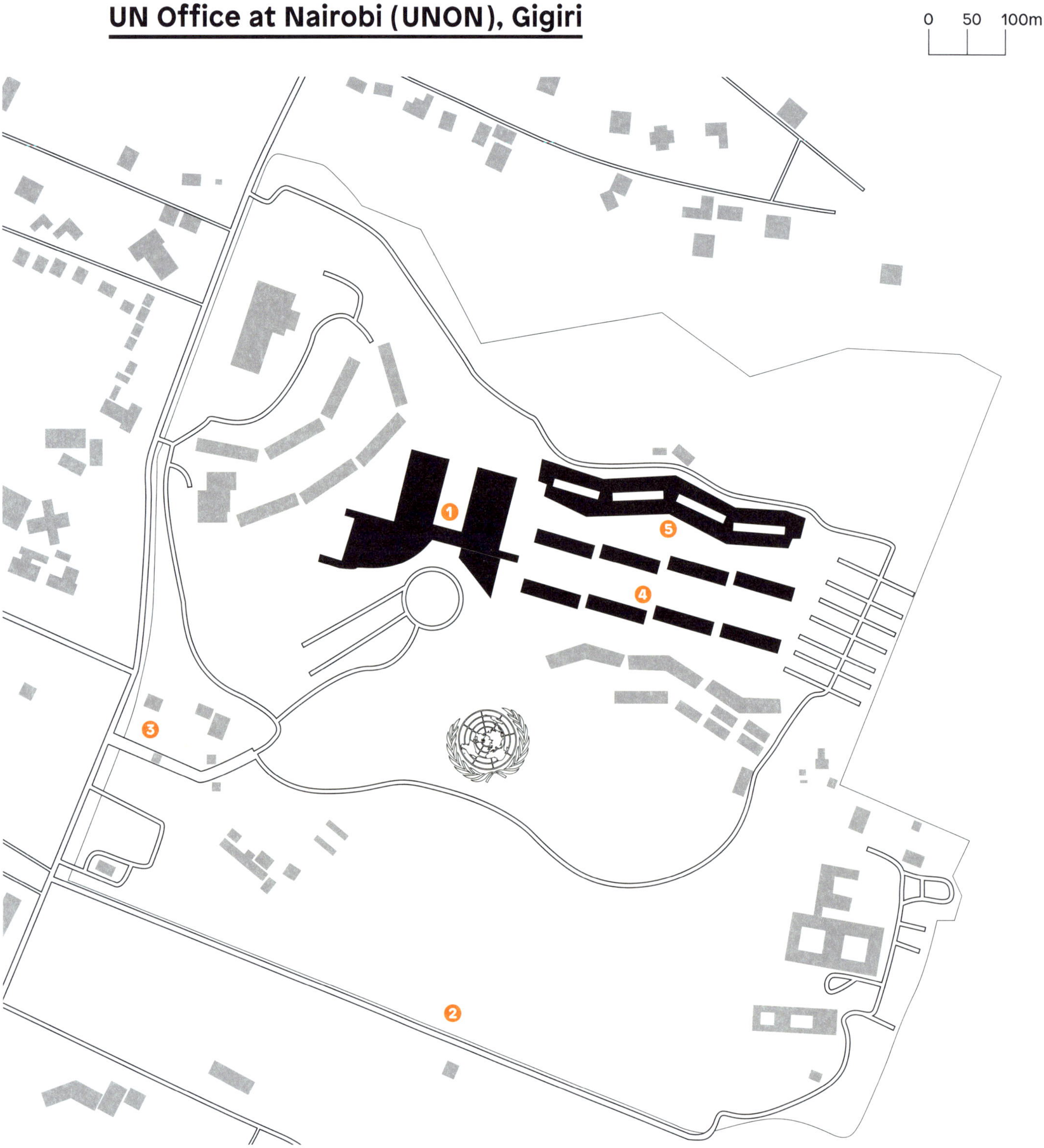

The UN's presence in Nairobi began in 1972, when the UN Environmental Programme (UNEP) established its global headquarters in Nairobi, the first top-level UN organization to have headquarters in the Third World. In 1976 the UN completed construction on the Gigiri complex on a property donated by the Kenyan Government. The Gigiri compound was originally built to house the global headquarters of UN-Habitat and UNEP. In 1996 it was officially inaugurated as one of four global headquarters for the UN, after New York, Geneva, and Vienna. Like the other UN headquarters, its site has extraterritorial status.

1

UNON Assembly Building

The UNON Assembly Building was designed by Kenya architect David Mutiso and opened in 1979. It houses the complex's main conference facilities.

2016.10.23

2

Perimeter wall

The wall separates UNON from the surrounding neighborhood and from the Karura Forest, which borders the complex to the east.

2004.03.13

2016.10.23

3

Main gate

The main entrance to the complex is off United Nations Avenue, directly across from the US embassy complex, which was built in 2003, after the bombing of the previous embassy in 1998.

2002.03.10

2016.10.23

4

Office blocks

These office blocks were part of the original group of buildings finished in 1979. They house the regional offices of many UN organizations, as well as regional offices for the World Food Programme and International Labor Organization.

2016.10.23

5

UN-Habitat and UNEP headquarters

The global headquarters of UN-Habitat and UNEP are accommodated in a net-zero carbon building, inaugurated in 2006. The building has interior courtyards, individually operable windows, and a large solar array to reduce its energy use.

2009.03.21

2009.10.12

2016.10.23

5.
Toward a Politics of Humanitarian Space

Writing about the relation of space to historical events, historian Karl Schlögel suggests that it is in the moment of the breakdown of the normal order that space, seemingly so self-evident as to be beyond mention, suddenly reappears and becomes newly visible to us, if only for a moment: "Space has been forgotten; it is barely there anymore. The frantic acceleration of our life, it is said, has made it disappear. Amid the smooth operation of our routines, it has virtually ceased to exist—at most, we catch a glimpse of it when these routines collapse: when catastrophe strikes, when our movements grind to an unscheduled halt. Then it is suddenly there: as a site, a crime scene, a disaster area. At such moments, our awareness returns that the world has its black holes—that, all acceleration notwithstanding, there is such a thing as geography, and it still matters."[1]

1 Karl Schlögel, *In Space We Read Time: On the History of Civilization and Geopolitics*, trans. Gerrit Jackson (New York: Bard Graduate Center, 2016), 7.

A disaster is a rupture in a spatial order that produces an awareness of the already spatial dimension of all social organization. Taking Schlögel's claim further, we might even suggest that disasters produce space, insofar as they destroy or disrupt previous spatial configurations and force new ones to be constructed. Perhaps this explains the importance of the idea of space in humanitarian operations—humanitarian space, as theorized by Rony Brauman—in that it is in the moment of crisis that the stability of space, the neutrality of the environment, and the fixity of its coordinates can no longer be taken for granted. Space ceases to be an invariant, a background, or a container; it becomes active, mobile, and operational, shrinking and growing in time according to a variable dimensionality determined by movements and actions rather than a preexisting grid. Humanitarian space cannot be assumed as a given, precisely because it is that space that appears when space is in crisis, when the spatial order itself becomes subjected to violence, whether political or environmental. It is within that reappearance of space itself, in the humanitarian crisis, that the neutral operational environment of humanitarian space must be established and defended.

If it is, as Schlögel suggests, that spatial orders become most recognizable at the moment they break down, an analysis of the spaces of humanitarian space should make apparent not only the spatiality of relief operations—the space of the black hole, in his words, into which the humanitarian steps—but also the texture of that space from which the black hole is torn: the operating logics of global institutions, national governments, and transnational capital. It is our hope that in describing the spaces of humanitarianism that their relation to the normal order, against which they seem to be an anomaly, can be better recognized. Humanitarian spaces are precisely not anomic, not outside the law; if they are a space of exception, to use Giorgio Agamben's term, they are nonetheless included in the nomos of international law and the globalized economy.[2] If anything, humanitarian space signals the delinking of sovereignty from the authority of the nation state, the opening up of a territory that is inscribed only in a multiscalar order, and is therefore not the lawless space of exception, but a form of emergent nonstate sovereignty.

2 Giorgio Agamben, *State of Exception*, trans. Kevin Attell (Chicago: University of Chicago Press, 2006).

In describing the architectural forms of international aid, we have tried to enrich the concept of humanitarian space by studying the physical artifacts that construct it, that build humanitarian space in the world. Humanitarian space is not only a theoretical conceit; rather, it has the weight, dimensions, and durability of the material facts that comprise it. It is animated, even as it is provisionally delimited, by a repertoire of checkpoints and border crossings, logistical hubs and EPZs, highways and ports. Attending to these particularities, the facts on the ground of humanitarian space, may help to capture the interplay between the universalizing mandate of humanitarianism and the concrete political and economic situations in which its operations take place—between the international order and its black holes.

Spatial Recursions

In studying the architectures of humanitarianism, we have attempted to identify certain patterns and consistencies in the repetition of spatial forms. While the physical attributes of each instance of a tower, wall, or park may differ or take on a local specificity, the repetition of these forms suggests a logic that exceeds their immediate situation. We have described these as typologies in keeping with the architectural lexicon, but another way of understanding them might be as recursions.

Recursion, as conceived by anthropologist Ann Laura Stoler, captures the sense of the serial reappearance of a figure that is always the same and yet also different. Stoler understands recursion as operating temporally, in the tendency of history to repeat itself, and sees the concept of a recursive history as moving beyond metaphors of either historical continuity or rupture.[3] As a corollary of Stoler's recursive history, we would also suggest a spatial recursion, the multiplication of spatial forms across geographical distance, where each instance is similar but nonetheless produces a different configuration of the surrounding space. The standard guard post unit used by the Israeli Defense Forces takes on different qualities and potentials when it is planted at an intersection, in a courtyard, on a rooftop, or atop a concrete barrier. The language of a law setting tariffs introduced in the wake of the Indian Ocean Tsunami in 2004 may be reused in legislation lowering duties on products from Haiti after the 2010 earthquake, but may produce an altogether different set of effects. In the repetition of a spatial form across varied local situations, it is possible to observe the ways in which it is always the same, always different; even when the physical or legal properties are identical, the recursive figure articulates a different set of relations and a new organization in each of the locales in which it touches down.

3 Ann Laura Stoler, *Duress: Imperial Durabilities in Our Times* (Durham: Duke University Press, 2016), 26.

Like the EPZ, nature preserve, refugee camp, or heritage site, the spatial recursions we consider are often a conjunction of the legal and the physical. To use a distinction proposed by architect Keller Easterling, they are an interplay of "object form" and "active form," both physical matter and operational protocol.[4] The spatial recursions of humanitarian space are active: they set in play, if not control, a series of possible effects, outcomes, or movements. Appreciating the activity of these forms in the ordering of humanitarian space is to recognize a potential agency in its reordering.

4 Keller Easterling, *Extrastatecraft: The Power of Infrastructure Space* (New York: Verso, 2014), 81–85.

A recursive analysis of the products of humanitarian space allows us to read the back and forth of the topologies that connect the global and local, universal and particular, moral and political-economic. Recursions after all are not just reappearances, but loops or circuits that traffic between familiar categories to create new and unexpected complexes: the nature reserve as land grab, the slum–national forest, or the humanitarian EPZ. In each of these hybrid forms, the appeal to universal good—whether of human life, environmental preservation, cultural heritage, or free trade—abets a much more ambiguous set of political and economic interrelations.

In the interest of recovering a moral ground against the determinations of the marketplace, architects and designers have sometimes embraced humanitarian claims of universality—the "four to five billion clients" of Architecture for Humanity's Cameron Sinclair. While such claims have the rhetorical advantage of shifting the justification and reception of the architect's work into a moral register, which may allow it to operate in domains where architects usually do not, we might recognize another set of potentials in the embeddedness of humanitarian space within recursive loops of political and economic interests operating across a range of scales. Far from sullying the self-evident benevolence of "social design" practices, giving attention to the political topologies of humanitarian space might open up new realms of practice for a certain kind of architect. Perhaps the drawings in this book can serve as the site plans, or existing conditions, in the drawing set of a possible future humanitarian architecture.

Humanitarian Temporalities

Humanitarian operations, as we have described, have a particular temporality. The state of emergency and the governmental powers it authorizes are justified as a temporary suspension of a normal order, a state of exception abetted by the urgency of the crisis. As Agamben has suggested, the spatial order that corresponds to the state of exception is the camp. The camp is built on the premise of its temporariness, the need to sustain a displaced or vulnerable population until the resolution of a conflict or resettlement after a disaster. But the duration of the crisis is indeterminate, and in some cases, such as in the

West Bank, can become quasi-permanent, relative to the scale of a human life, while remaining nominally provisional, oriented to a future that is always deferred. The suspension of politics in the moment of crisis then becomes an impediment to any political resolution.

The temporal dimension of humanitarian space is therefore a strategic point of entry for architectural and aesthetic practices. One project that works on the temporal protocols of humanitarian relief is the Concrete Tent in the Dheisheh camp, designed and constructed by Campus in Camps, led by architects Sandi Hilal and Alessandro Petti.[5] The structure, which takes the shape of a tent but is materialized in poured concrete, gives architectural form to the time of the permanent temporary, suspended between the pre-1948 past and an indeterminate future state. But it also provides a space for communal activities in the here-and-now. It creates an architectural fact on the ground in the immediate actuality of the building and the social relationships it supports. Without denying the permanent temporariness of the camp, now seventy years old, it creates a space for collective action in the present.

5 See the Concete Tent project at goo.gl/hgv6SZ.

The recent project Design for Legacy by architect Malkit Shoshan also works with the temporal scale of humanitarian operations. In collaboration with the leadership of the Dutch Ministry of Defense, which leads the UN peacekeeping mission in Mali, Shoshan designed a series of spatiotemporal protocols to guide the transformation in time of the typical UN peacekeeping base of operations.[6] Through a series of models, first shown at the 2016 Venice Architecture Biennale, Shoshan describes a process by which the infrastructure and facilities of the military base can be slowly integrated into the host community, first through interactions across the fence of the compound, then through the sharing of an intermediate space by the local people and the peacekeepers, and finally, once the mission ends, taking down the fence and turning over the use and maintenance of the base's structures to the civilian population. Shoshan acknowledges that the project runs the risk of abetting military interventions by burnishing their humanitarian credentials, but she argues that the afterlife of the base as a community space provides a much needed support for reconstructing social and civic life after a conflict.

6 See the project Design for Legacy at goo.gl/b7tBdM.

Humanitarian Scales

In invoking the name of humanity, humanitarianism always implies a scaling up from the immediate political and social relationships of a particular locality to the universal. It is a rhetorical operation that creates a scalar short circuit, in which some particular humans become humanity. The advantages of this strategy are evident, in that it allows the powerless to access a moral force that the state can only assert indirectly, through its own claims to a humanitarian purpose (for example, in providing housing or disaster relief), often with limited credibility.

Aesthetic projects can work on the variability of scales, exploring the potential reordering of the hierarchies of global / universal and local / particular, to insist on the possibility of new relationships between scales.

Laura Kurgan's work with satellite imagery, GIS, and remote sensing offers a possible direction beyond the hierarchies of scale and the nesting dolls of local, national, and global.[7] Her analysis of the proceedings of the International Criminal Tribunal for the former Yugoslavia (ICTY) in The Hague reveals the multiple scales and spaces, both physical and mediatic, through which the trial operated. The project demonstrates both the televisual scenography of the courtroom and the almost-real-time political effects of the broadcast. It describes a space into which human rights activists and activist architects could enter, the space of the short-circuit between the physical locality of the courtroom and the global media networks.

7 Laura Kurgan, *Close Up at a Distance: Mapping, Technology, and Politics* (New York: Zone Books, 2013).

Another example of work on scalar relations can be seen in the project Decolonize This Place by the artist collective MTL+. The project consisted of a series of events at Artists Space in New York over the course of three months in 2016, but it circulated more widely through a campaign of stickers that simply read, "Decolonize This Place." The sticker and its message could, of course, be applied to any place that the sticker-bearer thought appropriate. It made use of the universality of language—the fact that "this" marks a particular, but one that can be anything—to make visible the interrelatedness of indigenous, anticolonial, antigentrification, and global labor struggles. The project did not propose a humanitarian response to ongoing colonization, nor even one that recognized the human as a basis of commonality; rather, it sought to politicize places—all places—by calling attention to their continuing expropriation, and the need to mobilize communities founded on difference, not universality, to call for the repatriation of land.

Humanitarian Politics

Humanitarianism claims a moral purpose, in that it acts not in the interests of any parties, but for the good of humanity itself. In this sense, humanitarian morality could be seen as outside of or transcending political life. But humanitarian operations and their effects on cities are perhaps opposed not to the political, but to the state, and to the spatial ordering of the state in the institution of private property. Seen in this light, humanitarian spaces, like camps and settlements, might not be outside the polis; rather they are emergent forms of nonstate politics.

Recent scholarship on autonomy and "nonstate law" by anthropologists, such as Judith Scheele and Paul Dresch, has recognized the workings of law in the absence of a central power.[8] Humanitarian spaces might point toward new political formations, and property law and governance structures that are immanent to the refugee community. Community land trusts (CLTs) might provide a model for land tenure that respects the complex forms of ownership in refugee camps and communities where no land titles exist. In a CLT, rather than dividing parcels of land for individual ownership, the land is held in common. Decisions about land use and the allocation of spatial resources are made collectively, using decision-making structures set up by the community. CLTs have been advanced as a model in many different cities and contexts, including anti-gentrification struggles, public housing developments, community gardening networks, and efforts to protect land in rural communities. But they may be especially applicable to contexts where the land has never been divided into parcels, and where no legal distinction between public and private land exists, such as in Kibera and the Palestinian refugee camps. In that sense, they are a legal form that coincides with the actual social organization already existing in the slum or camp, rather than attempting to bring land under individual ownership and therefore into commodification. The politics of common land aligns with that of the slum and the refugee camp, a politics that points beyond private ownership and real estate speculation, toward a political community beyond the nation-state.

8 See, for example, Judith Scheele, "The Values of 'Anarchy': Moral Autonomy among Tubu-speakers in Northern Chad," *Journal of the Royal Anthropological Institute*, n.s., 21 (March 2015): 32–48; and Paul Dresch, "Aspects of Non-State Law: Early Yemen and Perpetual Peace," in *Legalism: Anthropology and History*, ed. Paul Dresch and Hannah Skoda (Oxford: Oxford University Press, 2012), 145–72.

Since the "movement of squares" of 2011 and after, we have seen a proliferation of networks of mutual aid and support in cities across the world, from cooperative businesses to radical mental health organizations and efforts to reclaim urban land for community uses. The task now is to affirm the bonds between these emergent forms of political organization and to claim their space as an existential territory of life in common. In the words of a letter from the occupiers of Tahrir Square, "It is not just the ideas that are important, these spaces are fundamental to the possibility of a new world."[9] To build these spaces requires imagining the architecture of a political community beyond the nation-state, a humanitarian architecture based not on the universal human reduced to bare life, but the human of a political life still to come.

9 A letter from the organizers of Tahrir Square to Occupy Wall Street, republished as "To the Occupy Movement: The Occupiers of Tahrir Square Are with You," *The Guardian*, October 25, 2011, goo.gl/3iCZBd.

Benedict Clouette, Marlisa Wise
FORMS OF AID
Architectures of Humanitarian Space

Copy editing: Keonaona Peterson
Project management: Katharina Kulke
Production: Katja Jaeger
Layout, cover design and typesetting:
Neeser & Müller
Paper: Plano Plus, 140g/m^2
Printing: Grafisches Centrum Cuno
GmbH & Co.KG, Calbe, printed in Ultra HD print

All drawings and photos by the authors.

Library of Congress Cataloging-in-Publication data
A CIP catalog record for this book has been applied for at the Library of Congress.

Bibliographic information published by the German National Library
The German National Library lists this publication in the Deutsche Nationalbibliografie; detailed bibliographic data are available on the Internet at http://dnb.dnb.de.

This publication is also available as an e-book
(ISBN PDF 978-3-0356-0826-7)

P.O. Box 44, 4009 Basel, Switzerland
Part of Walter de Gruyter GmbH, Berlin/Boston

Printed on acid-free paper produced from chlorine-free pulp. TCF ∞

Printed in Germany

ISBN 978-3-0356-1021-5

9 8 7 6 5 4 3 2 1

www.birkhauser.com

Acknowledgments:

We are grateful to the many organizations and individuals that have supported our research and writing throughout the development of this book.

We have been assisted by funding from the Graham Foundation for Advanced Studies in the Fine Arts and the Architectural League of New York, and we are thankful for the support of the staff at each organization. Columbia University also contributed funding to our research travel in the West Bank.

We have benefited from the brilliant community we found at Columbia, including Deans Mark Wigley and Amale Andraos, and Professors Barry Bergdoll, Laura Kurgan, Reinhold Martin, Mary McLeod, Mabel Wilson, and Gwendolyn Wright. Felicity Scott was especially supportive throughout our work on this project, first as an advisor on an early draft of the text and drawings and later as the director of the doctoral program in architectural history and theory at Columbia. Oskar Arnorsson and Eva Schreiner have also been enormously valuable interlocutors throughout the development of this work.

We are also thankful for our conversations and friendships with inspiring architects, artists, teachers, writers, and scholars, including Keller Easterling, Kian Goh, Jeffrey Inaba, Susan Jahoda, Stephen Korns, Leigh Claire La Berge, Diana Martinez, Malkit Shoshan, Susan Surface, Troy Therrien, Darien Williams, and Caroline Woolard.

Lastly, we wish to express our gratitude to the team at Birkhäuser who have guided this book to publication. Katharina Kulke and Alexander Felix have been patient and astute collaborators on this project. We are equally grateful for the elegant work of the graphic designers Neeser & Müller, and the careful copy editing of Keonaona Peterson.

This book is dedicated to our families: Bruce and Donna Clouette, and Kim Denney, Rich Jakshtis, Caroline Wise, and Sam Jakshtis. And to Io, soon to come.